W9-AWQ-981

THE HUMAN FUEL COOKBOOK

Also by **Health For Life**:

- **The Human Fuel Handbook**
  Nutrition for Peak Athletic Performance

- **Legendary Abs**

- **SynerAbs**

- **Transfigure I**
  9 Minutes to the Ultimate Buttocks and Thighs

- **Transfigure II**
  For the Ultimate Upper Body

- **Max O$_2$**
  A Synergistic Guide to Aerobic Training

- **The Health For Life Training Advisor**

- **SynerStretch:** For Whole Body Flexibility

- **SynerShape:** A Scientific Weight Loss Guide

- **Amino Acids and Other Ergogenic Aids**

- **Secrets of Advanced Bodybuilders**
  Synergistic Weight Training for the Whole Body

- **Secrets of Advanced Bodybuilders, Supplement #1**

- **The Weightless Workout**

ISBN 0-944831-29-X
Library of Congress Catalog Card Number: 93-79806

Health For Life
8033 Sunset Blvd., Suite 483 — Los Angeles, CA 90046 — (310) 306-0777

1 2 3 4 5 6 7 8 9

THE HUMAN FUEL COOKBOOK

Recipes for Peak Athletic Performance

by Ilene Caryn Simon, MPH

from Health For Life

For Liane

*CREDITS AND
ACKNOWLEDGMENTS*

Special thanks to
Harvey Karp, Dede Lipp,
Jerry Robinson, Janet Roston
Andrew Shields,
Jeff, Phyllis, and Stuart Simon,
Barry Weiss, and Harold Young.

Edited by Robert Miller
Book design by
Irene DiConti McKinniss
and Karl Shields
Illustrations by Leon Bach
Typesetting by Jack Hazelton,
Nutritional calculations by
Mark Hoffman

CONTENTS

4. PASTA AND GRAIN 43

WHO SAYS AN ATHLETE'S DIET HAS TO BE BORING?

In the quest for peak physical performance, it's clear that many athletes have given up hope of their diets actually providing any sort of pleasure. But take heart! **The Human Fuel Cookbook** proves that an athlete's diet need not be bland and repetitive. The recipes and menu plans in this book are designed to provide nutritionally sound, performance-enhancing meals that are *also* creative, delicious, and satisfying.

This cookbook is a companion volume to **The Human Fuel Handbook**, also published by Health For Life, and it abides by the basic nutritional principles defined there. Recipes are low in fat and sodium, and do not contain refined sugar or red meat. Most are high in energy-enhancing complex carbohydrates. And, to help you arrange your overall nutritional regimen, we've supplied detailed nutritional information at the end of every recipe.

Since we understand that time spent in the kitchen is time spent away from the gym, we've concentrated on recipes requiring little preparation time, and involving food items that are easily found in your supermarket or health food store.

Even if you're a novice in the kitchen, **The Human Fuel Cookbook** is for you. The sections entitled *The Athlete's Kitchen* and *The Athlete's Pantry* describe all of the basic tools and staple foods you'll need. In addition, throughout the book, you'll find instruction in basic cooking techniques. Trying new things in the kitchen may feel strange at first—as any physical skill may. But be persistent. As with athletics and martial arts, practice makes perfect. The results of your labor will be gratifying and delicious.

The primary food components of our human fuel recipes are whole grains, lean poultry and fish, and fresh fruits and vegetables. By choosing fresh, organic produce, poultry raised without chemical additives, and fresh fish caught in clean waters, you will guarantee the basic flavor and healthfulness of your food.

In these recipes, then, the flavors of foods are further enhanced with fresh herbs, citrus fruits, vinegars, and chicken or vegetable soup stock. Foods are healthfully prepared by steaming, baking, or grilling.

One small disclaimer. Occasionally a recipe may contain an ingredient traditionally thought of as taboo for the nutritionally conscious athlete. In moderation, though, these items will have very little impact on your nutritional status, and they can contribute enormously to the flavor and consistency of the meal. Below are a few examples.

BUTTER

Butter is a saturated fat, contains cholesterol and is therefore considered "bad for you." For years, margarine has been recommended as a healthy alternative. But the fact is, margarine has just about as much fat, contains the same number of calories as butter, and may also contain coloring agents and preservatives. Margarine's flavor is by all standards poor, and it reacts in an inferior way when you cook with it or use it in baking. For these reasons, some recipes in this cookbook use unsalted butter in small amounts.

More recipes, though, use olive or canola oil, and many boast *no fat* at all, making it quite possible to eat a large number of the meals in this book while still maintaining a strict, low-fat status. When a recipe calls for butter, we recommend using the certified, raw, unsalted variety, found in health food stores and many of the larger supermarket chains.

SALT

Too much salt can cause water retention and hypertension in some people. *Any* salt at all can be detrimental during the week prior to a bodybuilding contest. For these reasons, most recipes, when listing it as an ingredient, do not indicate an exact amount. All recipes can be prepared without any salt at all...but let's face it, a dash of salt can add a lot of flavor. Moderation is the key. Regular iodized table salt is chemically processed and adds a distinctively "chemical" flavor to foods. We recommend that you buy a French-made sea salt found in the gourmet section of the supermarket, or a domestic sea salt from the health food store.

HONEY

Honey is little more than liquid sugar. Still, most honey is made without chemical processing, and does offer some minimal nutritional value. Although many of the desserts in **The Human Fuel Cookbook** use fruit and fruit concentrates as sweetener, we found that some desserts just don't taste as good, and don't have as pleasing a consistency, without the addition of a little honey. Make sure to buy honey that is pure, raw, and unfiltered.

ALCOHOL

When you add wine or liquor to a recipe, the alcohol is evaporated and all that remains is its flavor…so it really isn't bad for you after all!

❖

Again, as with training, balance is key. We hope these recipes will provide you with a way to enjoy the pleasures of good food while reaping the full benefits of high-performance nutrition.

Happy training, and *bon appetit!*

❖   ❖   ❖

1

BASICS

THE ATHLETE'S KITCHEN

Trying to stock a kitchen with cooking tools and food essentials can be a confusing task. Department store shelves overflow with trendy gadgets and foodstuffs promising shortcuts to good nutrition—but many of the gadgets are just fads; and the foodstuffs, window dressing.

To prepare the recipes in this book, you need only the most basic supplies and tools. Buy the best quality you can afford, with an eye toward functionality rather than style. We recommend stainless steel pots with tight-fitting lids. All baking pans should be non-stick. Knives should be the best quality high-carbon stainless steel.

Pots and Pans

- 1-quart saucepan
- 2-quart saucepan
- 5-quart stockpot
- 6- to 8-quart stockpot for cooking soups and pasta
- 2 skillets or frying pans: 8 and 10 inches, preferably of a non-stick material like Silverston
- glass baking dish 13 x 9 x 2 inches
- 9-inch deep-dish pie plate
- loaf pan 9 x 5 x 3 inches
- square baking pan, 8 or 9 inches
- 12-cup muffin tin with ½-inch-deep cups
- cookie sheet
- collapsible vegetable steamer

Utensils

- set of glass or stainless steel mixing bowls
- set of measuring spoons
- set of measuring cups for dry ingredients
- 2-cup measuring cup for liquid ingredients
- hard rubber spatula
- flexible rubber spatula
- metal spatula
- soup ladle
- grater
- can/bottle opener
- vegetable peeler

- chopping board or surface
- long-handled wooden spoons
- long-handled metal spoon
- slotted stainless steel spoon
- colander
- zester
- sifter

- paring knife (approx. 4 inches)
- "cook's" or "chef's" knife (6 to 8 inches)
- serrated bread knife

Knives

- blender
- toaster oven
- ice cream maker
- Optional, but recommended:
  A food processor and/or electric hand mixer.

Equipment

THE ATHLETE'S PANTRY

What would you expect to find in the athlete's pantry? Some athletes feel that the healthiest diets are those with the fewest ingredients—and so they go for months, grimly facing the same boiled chicken at every meal. But our idea of high-performance nutrition is a bit different, and our cupboard is far from bare...

Imagine a cornucopia of healthful food basics upon which to build a varied and imaginative diet. By keeping a supply of the following basic food items on hand, you'll have most of what you need to put together tasty, nutritious meals in almost no time!

- basil
- bay leaf
- cinnamon
- cloves
- dill

Dry Herbs and Spices

- oregano
- ground black pepper (or better, whole peppercorns to grind as needed)
- rosemary
- sea salt
- seeds: poppy and sesame
- tarragon
- vanilla, extract and whole vanilla beans

Pantry Items

- baking powder
- baking soda
- beans: canned chickpeas, dried black, canned white bread crumbs
- broth, canned low-sodium chicken
- carob, chips and powder
- cereal grains: oatmeal, kashi, millet, etc.
- dried fruits: raisins, dates, apricots
- flours: whole wheat bread, whole wheat pastry, yellow cornmeal, oat bran
- honey: strained for cooking, unstrained for spreading
- mustard, whole grain
- nuts: almonds, pine nuts, walnuts, etc.
- nut butters: almond, and/or peanut, no sugar added
- oils: olive and canola
- pasta: whole wheat or artichoke, fresh and/or dried
- preserves, fruit sweetened
- protein powder
- rice: brown, wild
- soy sauce, low-sodium
- snacks: sports bars, rice cakes, etc..
- syrups: molasses, maple
- tea, herbal
- tuna, white meat, water-packed
- tomatoes: canned, high quality peeled, sliced or cut
- vinegar: a variety including balsamic, white-wine, tarragon, red-wine
- yeast, dry active

Refrigerated Goods

- butter, unsalted (keep in freezer)
- eggs, large
- fruit juice (for smoothies)
- milk, non-fat
- yogurt, non-fat

Note: Although it's good to always keep fresh—preferably organically grown—fruits and vegetables on hand, we suggest you buy perishable items as close as possible to the time you intend to cook and serve them.

❖   ❖   ❖

2

SOUPS

Carrot-Potato Soup

Serves 4
Prep time: 15 minutes
Cooking time: 30 minutes

Fresh-tasting and hearty, this soup is the perfect complement to a dinner of fresh grilled salmon. Top with chopped roasted red and green bell peppers for a dramatic visual effect.

1 pound carrots
1 russet potato
1 large yellow onion
1 cup chicken or clear vegetable broth
2 tablespoons chopped parsley
sea salt and ground black pepper to taste

1. Peel and chop vegetables. Simmer vegetables in broth, mixed with two cups of water, until vegetables are very soft.
2. Remove vegetables and broth from heat and allow to cool to room temperature.
3. Puree broth and vegetables, one cup at a time, in a blender or food processor.
4. Return pureed mixture to heat. Simmer until broth thickens, about 15 minutes over a low-medium heat. Add parsley.
5. Season with ground black pepper and salt if necessary. This soup may also be flavored with 3 tablespoons fresh, or 1 tablespoon dried, dill weed.

TOTAL CALORIES PER SERVING: 137

% Calories Carbohydrates: 82
% Calories Protein: 12
% Calories Fat: 5

Total Cholesterol: 0 mg.
Total Sodium: 265 mg.
Total Potassium: 899 mg.
Total Calcium: 76 mg.
Total Fiber: 4 gm.

Serve plain and simple, or add cooked rice or noodles, with steamed, chopped potatoes, celery, carrots, okra, squash, or any other vegetables you wish.

Chicken Soup

Serves 6
Prep time: 20 minutes
Cooking time: 1½ hours

2 2-pound chickens, or 1 4- to 5-pound hen, cut up in eight pieces.
3 stalks of celery, including leaves on the tops of stalks, whole
2 large carrots, peeled
1 parsnip, peeled
1 large onion, peeled
2 teaspoons salt
1 large clove garlic

1. Wash and clean chicken. Place in a large soup pot, and cover with cold water.
2. Cook over moderate heat to boil. Use a spoon to skim off foam that forms. Add vegetables and seasonings. Cover and cook on medium fire for 1 to 1½ hours, just until chicken is tender.
3. Allow soup to cool. Strain, and set chicken aside to use later for salads, or cut in chunks and return to soup. Carrots can also be sliced and returned to soup.
4. Put soup in refrigerator and chill overnight. Fat will solidify and should be removed before serving.
5. At this point, add any desired vegetables, rice, or noodles. Reheat to serve.

TOTAL CALORIES PER SERVING: 39

% Calories Carbohydrates: 2
% Calories Protein: 51
% Calories Fat: 47

Total Cholesterol: 1 mg.
Total Sodium: 776 mg.
Total Potassium: 210 mg.
Total Calcium: 9 mg.
Total Fiber: 0 gm.

Lentil Soup

Serves 6
Prep time: 30 minutes
Cooking time: 1 hour

The perfect cold-weather soup!

2 cups lentils
8 cups water
2 tablespoons extra virgin olive oil
4 garlic cloves, minced
1 large onion, peeled and chopped
4 celery stalks, sliced
2 carrots, peeled and sliced
1 8-ounce can stewed tomatoes, drained
4 tablespoons chopped fresh basil
2 tablespoons chopped cilantro
Balsamic vinegar and chopped parsley (optional)
sea salt and pepper to taste

1. Sauté lentils in olive oil, garlic, and onion for five minutes.
2. Add water and stewed tomatoes, and then celery, carrots, tomatoes, basil, and cilantro. Cover and cook over low heat for 1 hour.
3. Add salt and pepper to taste.
4. When you serve the soup, top with a teaspoon of vinegar and a teaspoon of chopped parsley.

TOTAL CALORIES PER SERVING: 153

% Calories Carbohydrates: 54
% Calories Protein: 18
% Calories Fat: 28

Total Cholesterol: 0 mg.
Total Sodium: 39 mg.
Total Potassium: 585 mg.
Total Calcium: 59 mg.
Total Fiber: 4 gm.

In this recipe, vegetables, soup stock, and pasta are cooked separately so that vegetables and pasta remain firm. Steaming the vegetables and adding them at the last minute also helps preserve their nutritional value.

1 yellow onion, peeled and finely chopped
1 cup chopped celery
¼ cup olive oil
1 28-ounce can chopped tomatoes
1 12-ounce can low-sodium chicken broth
1½ cups water
¼ cup chopped parsley
1 bay leaf
1 teaspoon dried, or 3 tablespoons chopped fresh, oregano
⅓ cup fresh basil leaves, chopped
½ teaspoon dried rosemary
½ cup chopped carrot
½ cup chopped zucchini
1 cup chopped broccoli
½ cup sliced mushrooms
½ cup chick-peas
½ cup whole wheat elbow macaroni, dry

1. Sauté onion, mushrooms, and celery in olive oil until onions are translucent and celery and mushrooms are soft.
2. Add tomatoes, chicken stock, and water. Add parsley and herbs, and season with sea salt and pepper if you wish. Simmer, covered, while preparing the vegetables.
3. Steam vegetables until tender but still firm.
4. Cook macaroni in boiling water until *al dente*.
5. Add chick-peas, vegetables, and macaroni to stock. Simmer for 5 minutes over low heat.

TOTAL CALORIES PER SERVING: 173

% Calories Carbohydrates: 50
% Calories Protein: 15
% Calories Fat: 35

Total Cholesterol: 0 mg.
Total Sodium: 293 mg.
Total Potassium: 820 mg.
Total Calcium: 109 mg.
Total Fiber: 3 gm.

Minestrone Soup

Makes 10 cups
Prep time: 30 minutes
Cooking time: 1 hour

Miso Soup

Makes 4 cups
Prep time: 10 minutes
Cooking time: 15 minutes

A high-protein, low-calorie soup with a distinctive Japanese flavor.

3½ cups water
1 package dashi (dashi, found in the asian food section of your market, is bouillon powder derived from bonito fish)
½ cup white or Japanese shiitake mushrooms, sliced
4 tablespoons red miso (found in the asian food section, miso is soybean paste)
⅔ cake tofu, cubed

Optional: 8 to 10 small fresh clams in the shell
¼ cup chopped green onions

1. Heat water over medium-high heat in a saucepan. Add dashi, and continue cooking for 5 minutes. Add mushrooms.
2. Remove 4 tablespoons liquid to a small bowl and stir in miso until combined. Return mixture to saucepan. Simmer over medium heat. Do not allow broth to boil after this point.
3. Add clams, and continue to cook until clams open. *Discard any clams that do not open.*
4. Add tofu and cook for two more minutes, until tofu is hot. Divide into bowls, and add green onion.

TOTAL CALORIES PER SERVING: 167

% Calories Carbohydrates: 34
% Calories Protein: 42
% Calories Fat: 24

Total Cholesterol: 29 mg.
Total Sodium: 1,308 mg.
Total Potassium: 400 mg.
Total Calcium: 100 mg.
Total Fiber: 1 gm.

This easy-to-prepare soup is filling and nutritious.

1 tablespoon olive oil
1 medium onion, minced
2 cloves chopped garlic
3 stalks minced celery
3 minced carrots
3 cups split peas
7 cups water
1 bay leaf
¼ teaspoon dried thyme

1. Saute onion, garlic, celery, and carrots in olive oil until tender.
2. Add water, bay leaf, and thyme.
3. Simmer in a large pot over a very low heat until peas are tender; about two hours.

TOTAL CALORIES PER SERVING: 192

% Calories Carbohydrates: 64
% Calories Protein: 21
% Calories Fat: 15

Total Cholesterol: 0 mg.
Total Sodium: 39 mg.
Total Potassium: 667 mg.
Total Calcium: 43 mg.
Total Fiber: 5 gm.

Split Pea Soup

Makes 5 cups
Prep time: 15 minutes
Cooking time: 2 hours

White Bean Stew

Serves 2
Prep time: 5 minutes
Cooking time: 10 minutes

Serve this stew with warm, crusty sourdough bread and a green salad. (Check the *Garlic Spinach* recipe on page 31 for additional instructions on preparing fresh spinach.)

1 tablespoon olive oil
1 bunch spinach, stems discarded
2 teaspoons fresh garlic, finely chopped
2 15-ounce cans white kidney beans, drained
1 12-ounce can stewed tomatoes, drained
freshly ground pepper to taste

1. Slice spinach into ½-inch strips.
2. Heat oil in large saucepan. Add garlic and spinach. Cook just until spinach wilts. Add tomatoes and beans. Cook until warm and serve.

TOTAL CALORIES PER SERVING: 466

% Calories Carbohydrates: 60
% Calories Protein: 23
% Calories Fat: 18

Total Cholesterol: 0 mg.
Total Sodium: 1,472 mg.
Total Potassium: 556 mg.
Total Calcium: 47 mg.
Total Fiber: 2 gm.

This soup is adapted from a recipe created by chef James Beard. Garbanzo beans are high in potassium, calcium, iron, and vitamin A—as well as great-tasting.

1 16-ounce can of garbanzo beans (chick-peas)
4 whole cloves garlic
⅓ cup olive oil
1½ teaspoon dried, crushed rosemary leaves
1 cup (12-ounce can) canned Italian tomatoes, chopped
1 cup canned chicken broth
freshly ground pepper to taste

1. Saute the garlic cloves in the olive oil over medium heat until browned. Remove from heat and allow to cool until lukewarm.
2. Add crushed rosemary to the oil, then the chopped tomatoes. Cook over a medium heat for 20 minutes. Stir frequently.
3. Add the drained chick-peas and cook for five more minutes. Add the broth and bring to boil.

TOTAL CALORIES PER SERVING: 511

% Calories Carbohydrates: 49
% Calories Protein: 12
% Calories Fat: 39

Total Cholesterol: 1 mg.
Total Sodium: 1448 mg.
Total Potassium: 902 mg.
Total Calcium: 139 mg.
Total Fiber: 5 gm.

Zuppa di Cici (Italian Garbanzo Bean Soup)

Serves 2 to 3
Prep time: 10 minutes
Cooking time: 20 minutes

3

SALADS AND VEGETABLES

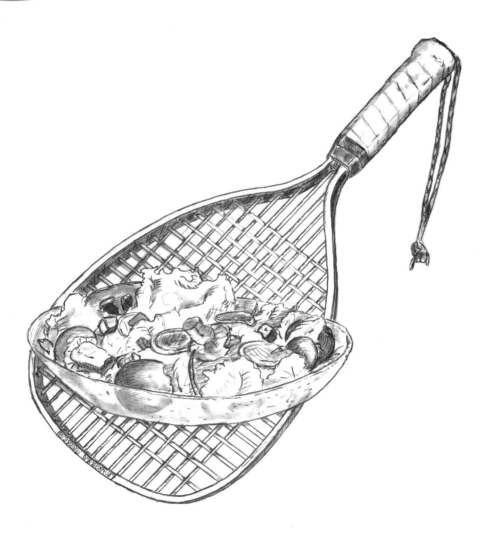

Ariel's Asian Pacific Salad

Serves 2
Prep time: 15 to 20 minutes

A refreshing, light salad, particularly well suited to a summer afternoon meal.

Salad:
½ red cabbage, shredded coarsely
½ cup fresh bean sprouts
½ cup Chinese snow peas
⅓ cake firm tofu, cut into bite-size cubes
¼ cup sliced almonds

Dressing:
1 tablespoon sesame oil
2 tablespoons rice vinegar

1. Toast almonds in oven by placing them in a shallow baking dish or cookie sheet and baking for 5 minutes at 350°. Almonds are done when they are golden brown in color. Set aside and cool.
2. In a large bowl, combine vegetables.
3. In a small bowl, mix oil and vinegar thoroughly.
4. Add tofu and dressing to salad. Toss lightly. Divide into two plates and top each with almonds.

TOTAL CALORIES PER SERVING: 349

% Calories Carbohydrates: 7
% Calories Protein: 22
% Calories Fat: 61

Total Cholesterol: 0 mg.
Total Sodium: 27 mg.
Total Potassium: 600 mg.
Total Calcium: 176 mg.
Total Fiber: 3 gm.

Fresh asparagus with a tart mustard sauce. Especially good in spring and early summer when asparagus comes into season.

½ pound fresh asparagus
1 tablespoon Dijon mustard
1 tablespoon sweet butter or olive oil

---

1. Prepare asparagus for cooking by breaking off tough bottoms of stalks and discarding them. They should snap off easily. Steam for 5 to 6 minutes.
2. In a small bowl, combine mustard and butter or olive oil. Mix until completely blended, using a fork or the back of a spoon.
3. Pour dressing over warm asparagus.

TOTAL CALORIES PER SERVING: 81

% Calories Carbohydrates: 12
% Calories Protein: 8
% Calories Fat: 80

Total Cholesterol: 0 mg.
Total Sodium: 132 mg.
Total Potassium: 154 mg.
Total Calcium: 23 mg.
Total Fiber: 0 gm.

Asparagus Dijonaise

Serves 2
Prep time: 10 minutes
Cooking time: 5 to 6 minutes

Broccoli Andrew

Serves 2 to 3
Prep time: 5 minutes
Cooking time: 10 minutes

Brighten up steamed broccoli with tangy balsamic vinegar and chewy, mildly sweet pine nuts.

3 cups broccoli florets
⅛ cup pine nuts
1 teaspoon dried oregano
¼ cup balsamic vinegar

1. Preheat oven to 350°.
2. Steam broccoli until firm, yet tender. This should take about 8 minutes.
3. Place pine nuts in a shallow baking pan in the oven for 5 to 7 minutes, or until pine nuts are lightly brown. Do not overcook.
4. In a large bowl or serving dish, toss warm broccoli with pine nuts, oregano, and balsamic vinegar.

TOTAL CALORIES PER SERVING: 123

% Calories Carbohydrates: 33
% Calories Protein: 17
% Calories Fat: 51

Total Cholesterol: 0 mg.
Total Sodium: 48 mg.
Total Potassium: 530 mg.
Total Calcium: 76 mg.
Total Fiber: 2 gm.

Broiled Potatoes

Oil can be deleted during a pre-race diet or to create a filling and fat-free side dish.

6 small red potatoes
6 tablespoons virgin olive oil
2 cloves garlic, minced
sea salt to taste
freshly ground black pepper

Serves 2
Prep time: 10 minutes
Cooking time: 15 to 20 minutes

1. Slice the potatoes in quarters. Steam them in a vegetable steamer on stovetop until potatoes are firm, but tender (about 10 to 12 minutes).
2. Set potatoes in a square baking dish, with the insides of the potatoes facing up. Make a small cut crosswise in the center of each piece. Spread garlic and olive oil on potatoes.
3. Set the baking dish under the broiler until potatoes are crisp and golden brown (about 5 to 7 minutes). Season to taste.

TOTAL CALORIES PER SERVING: 536

% Calories Carbohydrates: 72
% Calories Protein: 6
% Calories Fat: 22

Total Cholesterol: 0 mg.
Total Sodium: 146 mg.
Total Potassium: 307 mg.
Total Calcium: 103 mg.
Total Fiber: 1 gm.

Tangy Carrot Salad

Serves 2
Prep time: 15 minutes

Carrots are lightly accented with spicy cumin and sweet-tart raspberry vinegar.

Salad:
1½ cups carrots, peeled and shredded
½ tablespoon cumin (Dried cumin can be found in the spice section of your grocery or health food store.)

Dressing:
¼ cup olive oil
5 tablespoons raspberry vinegar

1. Combine carrots and cumin in large bowl.
2. In a small cup or bowl, mix oil and vinegar. Stir vigorously to combine ingredients completely.
3. Combine carrots and dressing, and chill.

TOTAL CALORIES PER SERVING: 149

% Calories Carbohydrates: 20
% Calories Protein: 2
% Calories Fat: 79

Total Cholesterol: 0 mg.
Total Sodium: 20 mg.
Total Potassium: 189 mg.
Total Calcium: 19 mg.
Total Fiber: 1 gm.

Snow peas are flat and crunchy. They are a delicious alternative to the plain round-shell peas usually served with carrots. This vegetable dish goes well with fish or poultry.

½ pound snow peas, ends trimmed and strings removed
½ pound carrots, peeled and sliced in julienne
2 shallots, peeled and sliced
1 teaspoon unsalted butter
1 tablespoon fresh, or 1 teaspoon dried, dill

1. Steam carrots and snow peas until tender, about 5 to six minutes. (Note: Snow peas will cook faster than carrots, so add them after the carrots have steamed for several minutes.)
2. While vegetables are steaming, melt butter in a small saucepan, and saute shallots until translucent and tender, about 5 to 7 minutes.
3. Transfer peas and carrots to serving dish. Toss with shallots and dill.

TOTAL CALORIES PER SERVING: 216

% Calories Carbohydrates: 70
% Calories Protein: 18
% Calories Fat: 12

Total Cholesterol: 6 mg.
Total Sodium: 60 mg.
Total Potassium: 892 mg.
Total Calcium: 97 mg.
Total Fiber: 8 gm.

Chinese Snow Peas and Carrots with Dill

Serves 2
Prep time: 10 minutes
Cooking time: 10 minutes

Crunchy Raw Vegetable Salad

Serves 2
Prep time: 20 minutes

This salad may be eaten as a side dish, or stuffed inside a whole wheat pita pocket with yogurt or cheese as a sandwich.

1 carrot
1 green bell pepper
1 red bell pepper
1 small bunch of radishes
any of the following: celery, cauliflower, broccoli, cucumber, fresh green beans, scallions, or zucchini

1. Dice all vegetables into bite-size pieces (about ½-inch chunks)
2. Serve with yogurt, a vinaigrette or yogurt dressing, or plain with a bit of lemon squeezed on top.

TOTAL CALORIES PER SERVING: 130

% Calories Carbohydrates: 50
% Calories Protein: 9
% Calories Fat: 41

Total Cholesterol: 0 mg.
Total Sodium: 51 mg.
Total Potassium: 918 mg.
Total Calcium: 95 mg.
Total Fiber: 4 gm.

Yogurt flavored with herbs and garlic enhances the flavor of crisp cucumbers.

2 7- to 8-inch, or one English, or hot-house, cucumber
¾ cup plain non-fat yogurt
1 small clove garlic, crushed
2 fresh mint leaves, minced
1 teaspoon dried dill
salt and pepper to taste

1. Slice and halve cucumbers. If they are waxed, peel them first.
2. Combine with the rest of the ingredients, then chill.

TOTAL CALORIES PER SERVING: 104

% Calories Carbohydrates: 56
% Calories Protein: 14
% Calories Fat: 30

Total Cholesterol: 11 mg.
Total Sodium: 241 mg.
Total Potassium: 656 mg.
Total Calcium: 177 mg.
Total Fiber: 0 gm.

Cucumber Salad

Serves 2
Prep time: 15 minutes

French String Beans à la Shields

Serves 2
Prep time: 10 minutes
Cooking Time: 5 to 7 minutes

The classic combination of string beans and toasted almonds is prepared here with less fat, and flavored with lemon in place of salt for increased healthfulness. It can be served hot or at room temperature.

2 cups string beans, diagonally cut into 1½-inch segments
¼ cup sliced or slivered almonds
3 tablespoons lemon juice
1 tablespoon unsalted butter or olive oil (optional)

1. Preheat oven to 350°.
2. Steam string beans about 5 minutes, until tender but still crisp.
3. Place almonds in shallow baking dish and toast in oven until lightly brown, about 5 to 7 minutes.
4. In a medium bowl, toss string beans with almonds, lemon juice, and butter or olive oil. Serve immediately.

TOTAL CALORIES PER SERVING: 235

% Calories Carbohydrates: 27
% Calories Protein: 11
% Calories Fat: 62

Total Cholesterol: 6 mg.
Total Sodium: 8 mg.
Total Potassium: 590 mg.
Total Calcium: 139 mg.
Total Fiber: 3 gm.

A simple vegetable dish that is the perfect complement to any pasta main course.

1 package prewashed spinach leaves or two small bunches spinach
2 cloves garlic, finely chopped
2 tablespoons olive oil

---

1. Re-rinse prewashed spinach—or thoroughly wash and dry spinach leaves to remove all dirt.
2. In a large skillet, heat olive oil over medium heat. Add garlic, and saute for 5 minutes until lightly brown. Add spinach leaves. Mix well, reduce heat and cover for 2 minutes. Remove cover and stir over heat for another 2 to 3 minutes. Serve immediately.

TOTAL CALORIES PER SERVING: 147

% Calories Carbohydrates: 13
% Calories Protein: 9
% Calories Fat: 79

Total Cholesterol: 0 mg.
Total Sodium: 89 mg.
Total Potassium: 636 mg.
Total Calcium: 117 mg.
Total Fiber: 4 gm.

Garlic Spinach

Serves 2
Prep time: 15 minutes

Grilled Salad

Serves 2
Prep time: 45 minutes

A delicious main dish salad, adapted from the elegant Ivy at the Shore restaurant in Santa Monica, California—just a few miles north of Golds and World gyms. Those exiled to colder climates might try serving this simple recipe at home, and see if you don't feel the breeze roll in off the Pacific.

½ dozen large shrimp, peeled
½ chicken breast, boned and sliced into 1-inch strips
½ dozen asparagus spears, sliced into 1½-inch pieces
½ avocado, cut into bite-size pieces
1 zucchini, sliced
8 cherry tomatoes, sliced in half
2 large carrots, peeled and sliced
4 cups salad greens (Any mix of romaine, green leaf, and red leaf lettuce is acceptable—or try mixed baby lettuces if they are available at your market.)

1. Marinate shrimp, sliced chicken breast, asparagus, and zucchini in white-wine or balsamic vinaigrette (see Chapter 12).
2. In a large bowl, mix greens, carrots, and tomatoes.
3. Place chicken, shrimp, asparagus, and zucchini on a barbecue or gas grill. You may use your oven broiler, but you will lose the flavor you get from charcoal or wood.
4. Remove each ingredient from grill when it is cooked. Expect vegetables and shrimp to be done several minutes before the chicken. Allow ingredients to cool to room temperature.
5. Add grilled ingredients to salad, add avocado, and toss with Balsamic Vinaigrette from page 132.
6. Divide between two large plates, and serve.

TOTAL CALORIES PER SERVING: 506

% Calories Carbohydrates: 18
% Calories Protein: 18
% Calories Fat: 64

Total Cholesterol: 69 mg.
Total Sodium: 167 mg.
Total Potassium: 1,535 mg.
Total Calcium: 117 mg.
Total Fiber: 4 gm.

Grilled Tomatoes

A quick and easy complement to any main dish. The flavor of this dish depends largely on the quality of the tomatoes. For best results, use firm, ripe, organically grown tomatoes.

Serves 2
Prep time: 10 minutes
Cooking time: 10 minutes

2 large beefsteak tomatoes, sliced in half crosswise
4 tablespoons bread crumbs
2 teaspoons finely chopped Italian parsley
2 teaspoons butter or olive oil

1. Preheat oven to 425°.
2. Sprinkle equal amounts of bread crumbs, parsley, and butter on each tomato half.
3. Bake 10 minutes or until toppings are brown and crispy.

TOTAL CALORIES PER SERVING: 96

% Calories Carbohydrates: 48
% Calories Protein: 10
% Calories Fat: 43

Total Cholesterol: 11 mg.
Total Sodium: 132 mg.
Total Potassium: 361 mg.
Total Calcium: 29 mg.
Total Fiber: 2 gm.

Tossed Green Salad with Jicama and Tangerines

Serves 2
Prep time: 15 minutes.

This salad can easily be served as a main dish by adding sliced, grilled or broiled chicken breast. For special occasions, add ⅛ to ¼ cup of edible flowers. Pansies and nasturtiums are both edible, and can sometimes be found in the gourmet sections of larger markets. You can also take them right from your fall or spring garden! They are quite tasty and look beautiful in the salad.

1 small head butter or limestone lettuce
½ pound jicama, peeled, and sliced julienne-style or cut into bite-size chunks
2 small tangerines, peeled, seeds and white membranes removed, and sectioned
2 scallions, sliced
Lime-Dill Dressing (p. 127), or White-Wine Vinaigrette (p. 133)

1. Remove lettuce leaves from head, wash and dry carefully.
2. Combine lettuce, jicama, tangerines, and scallions in a large salad bowl.
3. Toss with vinaigrette.
4. Divide between two plates, and sprinkle with flowers.

TOTAL CALORIES PER SERVING: 197

% Calories Carbohydrates: 73
% Calories Protein: 14
% Calories Fat: 13

Total Cholesterol: 0 mg.
Total Sodium: 28 mg.
Total Potassium: 1,401 mg.
Total Calcium: 34 mg.
Total Fiber: 4 gm.

The ultimate "comfort food!"

1 pound White Rose potatoes
½ teaspoon salt
¾ cup buttermilk or skim milk
2 teaspoons unsalted butter
freshly ground pepper, to taste

1. Peel potatoes and place in a medium-size saucepan. Cover potatoes with water and bring to boil over high heat. Reduce heat, and continue to cook until potatoes are tender—about 15 to 30 minutes, depending on their size.
2. Place potatoes in a large bowl and mash with a fork until mostly smooth. (If you like, leave a few lumps to create more texture.)
3. Add milk and beat with a wooden spoon until liquid is thoroughly incorporated. Stir in butter and serve.

TOTAL CALORIES PER SERVING: 296

% Calories Carbohydrates: 73
% Calories Protein: 12
% Calories Fat: 15

Total Cholesterol: 14 mg.
Total Sodium: 211 mg.
Total Potassium: 1,673 mg.
Total Calcium: 132 mg.
Total Fiber: 10 gm.

Low-Fat Mashed Potatoes

Serves 2 to 3
Prep time: 15 minutes
Cooking time: 15 to 30 minutes

Minted Peas

Serves 2
Prep time: 10 minutes
Cooking time: 10 minutes

A fresh and satisfying dish when prepared without fat or salt. May be served hot or at room temperature.

1 pound fresh, unshelled peas (to yield 1 cup shelled peas) or 1-pound package of frozen green peas
1 tablespoon unsalted butter or extra virgin olive oil
1 tablespoon fresh mint, chopped
sea salt and freshly ground pepper to taste

1. Shell fresh peas. Steam fresh or frozen peas until bright green and tender but not soggy, about 10 to 12 minutes.
2. In a serving bowl, toss prepared peas with mint, oil or butter, sea salt, and pepper.

TOTAL CALORIES PER SERVING: 180

% Calories Carbohydrates: 63
% Calories Protein: 23
% Calories Fat: 14

Total Cholesterol: 6 mg.
Total Sodium: 206 mg.
Total Potassium: 513 mg.
Total Calcium: 62 mg.
Total Fiber: 7 gm.

Nicoise Salad

Serve this main course salad with crusty bread for a light Mediterranean-style summer meal.

Serves 2
Prep time: 30 minutes

4 medium-sized "new" red potatoes (approximately ½ pound)
1 pound green beans
4 fresh Italian plum tomatoes, halved and sliced
2 hard-boiled eggs, shelled and quartered (yolks can be left out to reduce fat and calorie content)
1 6-ounce can white meat tuna, drained
¼ cup pitted and halved Nicoise olives
4 anchovy fillets (optional)
1 small head of butter lettuce
Balsamic Vinaigrette Dressing (p. 134)

1. Boil potatoes in salted water for 10 minutes. Potatoes should be cooked but still firm. Cool. Cut potatoes in quarters.
2. Steam green beans until tender. Be careful not to overcook. Cool.
3. Arrange lettuce leaves on a plate. Flake tuna and place in the center. Arrange eggs, olives, green beans, tomatoes, anchovies, and olives around tuna.
4. Pour Balsamic Vinaigrette over salad and serve.

TOTAL CALORIES PER SERVING: 491

% Calories Carbohydrates: 52
% Calories Protein: 33
% Calories Fat: 15

Total Cholesterol: 274mg.
Total Sodium: 520 mg.
Total Potassium: 2,816 mg.
Total Calcium: 138 mg.
Total Fiber: 5 gm.

Potato, Corn, and Pepper Salad

Serves 2
Prep time: 45 minutes

The sweet flavors of red peppers and summer corn perfectly complement the hearty taste and consistency of potatoes. A great dish to serve at a barbecue.

5 small new potatoes
1 ears of yellow corn
½ red bell pepper
½ green bell pepper
¼ cup White-Wine or Balsamic Vinaigrette
leaves from 1 large sprig of tarragon
freshly ground black pepper, to taste

1. Cut new potatoes into quarters. Steam until cooked but still firm.
2. Steam corn for five minutes. Shear corn off ear. Combine in bowl with potatoes, and allow to cool.
3. Roast bell peppers on stovetop (see box on next page), peel, and slice into narrow 2-inch strips. Combine with potatoes and corn.
4. Combine oil and vinegar, stir vigorously. Toss with salad. Chill and serve.

TOTAL CALORIES PER SERVING: 334

% Calories Carbohydrates: 72
% Calories Protein: 9
% Calories Fat: 20

Total Cholesterol: 0 mg.
Total Sodium: 26 mg.
Total Potassium: 1,690 mg.
Total Calcium: 30 mg.
Total Fiber: 15 gm.

Leeks are a fragrant root vegetable that taste like a very mild, sweet red onion, and look a lot like a large scallion.

2 potatoes, peeled and sliced paper-thin
1 leek (use only white bulb and ½ inch of green)
⅓ cup low-sodium chicken broth
1 egg white
sea salt and pepper to taste

1. Preheat oven to 350°.
2. In a 9-inch baking dish lightly coated with olive oil, combine potatoes, leeks, chicken broth, and egg white.
3. Bake for 40 to 45 minutes. Mixture should be lightly browned and crispy on the top.

TOTAL CALORIES PER SERVING: 113

% Calories Carbohydrates: 79
% Calories Protein: 18
% Calories Fat: 3

Total Cholesterol: 0 mg.
Total Sodium: 356 mg.
Total Potassium: 702 mg.
Total Calcium: 23 mg.
Total Fiber: 4 gm.

Roasted Potatoes with Leeks

Serves 2
Prep time: 10 minutes
Cooking time: 45 minutes

TO ROAST PEPPERS...

Char the skin of any bell pepper by placing it directly on top of a gas burner or barbecue until the skin is black and crackly all over. Remove from heat and place in a closed brown paper bag for 15 minutes. This will steam the pepper. Remove from bag and peel the skin of the pepper away with the dull side of a butter knife or with your hands. It's OK. if a small amount of skin remains. Slice the pepper in half, and scrape off the seeds. Do not rinse with water.

Simple Ratatouille

Serves 2
Prep time: 40 minutes
Cooking time: 20 minutes

This is a richly flavored dish with a Mediterranean flair. If you like your food spicy, add ½ teaspoon red pepper flakes. Serve over brown rice, millet, or pasta.

1 tablespoon olive oil
1 yellow onion, medium, sliced
2 cloves garlic, chopped
2 medium zucchini, sliced
2 Japanese eggplants, sliced
1 12-ounce can stewed tomatoes
¼ cup chopped parsley
2 cloves garlic, chopped
1 teaspoon dried oregano
1 teaspoon dried basil
sea salt and pepper to taste

1. Heat the olive oil in a large skillet. Add garlic and onion. Saute for five minutes, or until onion is translucent and tender.
2. Add the remainder of the ingredients. Reduce heat and cover. Cook for another 20 to 25 minutes, stirring occasionally. Serve hot or cold.

TOTAL CALORIES PER SERVING: 321

% Calories Carbohydrates: 50
% Calories Protein: 11
% Calories Fat: 39

Total Cholesterol: 0 mg.
Total Sodium: 472 mg.
Total Potassium: 2,155 mg.
Total Calcium: 324 mg.
Total Fiber: 5 gm.

A simple, elegant, low-calorie main dish salad.

Salad:
½ pound large cooked shrimp, peeled
1 small head of butter lettuce
1 small red bell pepper, cut in thin strips
2 scallions, sliced

Dressing:
½ cup plain non-fat yogurt
1 tablespoon plus 1 teaspoon Dijon mustard
1 tablespoon white-wine vinegar
2 teaspoon honey

1. Wash and dry butter lettuce. Tear into bite-size pieces and arrange on two large dinner plates
2. Arrange shrimp, bell pepper and scallions on top.
3. Mix yogurt, mustard, white-wine vinegar, and honey in a medium-size bowl, and stir vigorously until ingredients are combined completely. Toss with salad.

TOTAL CALORIES PER SERVING: 486

% Calories Carbohydrates: 34
% Calories Protein: 31
% Calories Fat: 35

Total Cholesterol: 202 mg.
Total Sodium: 371 mg.
Total Potassium: 38,800 mg.
Total Calcium: 188 mg.
Total Fiber: 2 gm.

Shrimp Salad with Honey-Mustard Dressing

Serves 2
Prep time: 15 minutes

Vegetable and Tofu Stir-Fry on Soba Noodles

Serves 2
Prep time: 20 minutes
Cooking time: 10 minutes

Japanese soba noodles are made from buckwheat and wheat flours. They cook faster than American whole grain pasta and have a more delicate consistency. Their distinctive taste blends perfectly with this vegetable and tofu combination.

½ 10-ounce package whole wheat soba noodles
½ yellow onion, peeled and sliced into thin strips
3 cups broccoli, cut into florets
1 red bell pepper, cut into thin strips
2 carrots, peeled and cut into thin diagonal slices
1 cup fresh white mushrooms, sliced
⅓ cake firm tofu
1 clove garlic, minced
1 inch piece of fresh ginger, peeled and minced
1 tablespoon sesame oil
1 tablespoon low-sodium soy sauce
1 tablespoon cooking sherry
2 tablespoons sesame seeds
¼ teaspoon salt

1. Fill a soup pot with cold water and ¼ teaspoon salt, and bring to a boil. Add soba noodles. Cook noodles *al dente,* about 7 to 8 minutes, then remove and drain.
2. In a large frying pan or wok, heat sesame oil over a high flame. Add onion, carrots, ginger, and garlic. Stir. After 30 seconds, add broccoli. Stir and then cover for 2 minutes. Stir again and add mushrooms. Sprinkle about a teaspoon of water, plus the soy sauce and sherry, on the top, cover pan, and cook for 2 more minutes. Add tofu, and stir gently. Remove from heat.
3. Divide noodles between two plates, and top with vegetables & tofu. Sprinkle with sesame seeds; serve.

TOTAL CALORIES PER SERVING: 316

% Calories Carbohydrates: 42
% Calories Protein: 17
% Calories Fat: 41

Total Cholesterol: 0 mg.
Total Sodium: 1,723 mg.
Total Potassium: 1,005 mg.
Total Calcium: 173 mg.
Total Fiber: 4 gm.

4

PASTA AND GRAIN

ABOUT GRAINS

Whole grains are a nutritional mainstay for athletes and bodybuilders. They contain proteins, fats, carbohydrates, and fiber, as well as vitamins and minerals essential to maintaining peak performance. Simple preparation is described below, and is the basis for many of the recipes in this book. The addition of vegetables, fish, poultry, herbs, and spices makes for performance-enhancing, flavorful meals. Be creative!

Barley

We recommend adding cooked barley to soups and stews. To cook whole barley, add 1 cup barley to 3 cups water. Cook over low heat for 1 hour.

Bulgur Wheat

Bulgur has been steamed, dried, and cracked into small pieces. It is commonly used in Middle Eastern cooking, and can be found in our tabbouleh recipe on page 60. Since it has been precooked, it can be prepared quickly. Pour two cups of boiling water over 1 cup of bulgur wheat, cover, and let stand at room temperature for 20 minutes.

Buckwheat

Buckwheat is actually an edible fruit seed related to rhubarb. As buckwheat is a fine grain with a low gluten content, it is most often mixed together with wheat flour in cooking. Baked products made with buckwheat alone tend to fall apart. Toasted buckwheat is known as kasha, and is featured in our recipe for cold Kasha Salad on page 49. To cook, add 1 cup buckwheat to 2 cups boiling water. Reduce heat and cover. Simmer for 15 to 20 minutes.

Couscous

Couscous is actually a pasta product made from semolina, a refined wheat product. The flour is ground, mixed with water, and formed into thin strands. The strands are then broken into tiny pieces, steamed, and dried. To find more nutrient-rich, non-refined couscous may require a trip to your local healthfood store. Preparation is easy and fast! Add $1\frac{1}{2}$ cups boiling water to 1 cup couscous. Cover and allow to stand at room temperature for 15 minutes.

Millet

Millet holds the distinctions of being the most easily digestable of all grains and of having a particularly high protein content, making it an ideal pre-contest food. Add 2½ cups water to 1 cup millet. Cook over a low heat for 30 minutes.

Oats

Athletes and bodybuilders have long started the day with a steaming bowl of plain, hot oatmeal. This makes good nutritional sense, given the cholesterol-lowering effects of oat bran. Regular and quick-cooking varieties do not differ in nutritional value, but regular oats do have a more satisfying consistency and are worth the cooking time if you have it available. To cook regular rolled oats, boil 2½ cups water, add 1 cup oats, stir for 2 to 3 minutes, cover, and cook over low heat for 15 minutes.

Rice

Rice is the most widely consumed staple food in the world. White rice, from which the nutritious bran and germ layers have been removed, is a nutritionally inferior food, consisting almost entirely of starch. Conversly, all forms of brown rice provide an excellent source of B vitamins, calcium, phosphorous, Vitamin E, iron, and fiber. To prepare rice, combine 2 cups water with 1 cup rice. Bring them to a boil in an uncovered pot. Once a rapid boil has been reached, cover, and cook over very low heat for 45 minutes.

Wild Rice

Wild rice is not actually rice at all, but rather the fruit seed of a tall aquatic grass. It has a nutty taste and is delicious served cold, as the basis of a salad, or warm with fish or poultry. To cook, add 4 cups of water to 1 cup wild rice. Cook over low heat in a covered saucepan for 45 to 55 minutes.

Wheat

Nutritionally speaking, the difference between whole products and white, processed products is profound. Unbleached white flours have been stripped of bran and germ layers. Bleached all-purpose flours have been processed with dough conditioners and preservatives, and have had vitamins added in an effort to restore some of the lost nutritional value. In general, our recipes use whole wheat pastry or whole wheat bread flour. There is a significant difference in consistency between the two, so please take note of the distinction. Sometimes we will add a small amount of unbleached white flour to lighten the consistency or improve the taste of a dish. It is always fine to substitute whole wheat flour for nutritional reasons, but be aware it will alter the taste and consistency by making a product heavier and giving it a stronger, more "wheaty" flavor.

Angel Hair Pasta with Tomatoes, Basil, Garlic, and Olive Oil

Serves 2
Prep time: 25 minutes

This is an easy, quick-to-prepare pasta dish. It involves the use of only one pot because the sauce is never cooked—just quickly heated by the pasta itself.

1 pound ripe Roma tomatoes, peeled and seeded
3 tablespoons best quality olive oil
8 fresh basil leaves, coarsely chopped
3 cloves garlic, finely chopped
½ pound whole grain angel hair pasta

1. Boil water for pasta.
2. Dice tomatoes into small pieces. Combine with basil and garlic. Add olive oil and toss. Allow to rest at room temperature.
3. Cook pasta according to package directions until *al dente*.
4. Toss pasta and sauce in large bowl. Serve.

TOTAL CALORIES PER SERVING: 523

% Calories Carbohydrates: 45
% Calories Protein: 7
% Calories Fat: 48

Total Cholesterol: mg.
Total Sodium: 12 mg.
Total Potassium: 381 mg.
Total Calcium: 104 mg.
Total Fiber: 2 gm.

Risotto should be served *al dente*—you should be able to "bite" into the inside of the rice even though the outside is very creamy. This dish is traditionally made with Italian arborio rice, and although you can use regular short-grain brown rice for this dish, the consistency will be far less delicate.

1 cup asparagus spears, sliced into 1-inch pieces
¼ cup Italian parsley, chopped, packed tightly
1 teaspoon dried oregano
1 small carrot
½ yellow onion
1 clove garlic
1 tablespoon sweet butter
3 tablespoons olive oil
2¼ cups chicken or vegetable stock
1 cup drained canned chopped tomatoes
1 cup Italian arborio rice
salt and pepper to taste

1. Finely chop carrot, garlic, and onion. Slice asparagus.
2. Heat butter and oil in saucepan over medium heat. When butter is melted, add chopped ingredients and asparagus; stir constantly for 2 minutes.
3. Add rice and oregano, and saute for 4 more minutes.
4. At the same time, heat broth and tomatoes until they reach a boil.
5. Add broth, just a little at a time, and stir gently. Do not add more broth until rice has absorbed the broth completely. This should take about 20 minutes. When broth is absorbed, add salt and freshly ground black pepper to taste. Serve immediately.

TOTAL CALORIES PER SERVING: 704

% Calories Carbohydrates: 53
% Calories Protein: 9
% Calories Fat: 38

Total Cholesterol: 18 mg.
Total Sodium: 2,062 mg.
Total Potassium: 1,162 mg.
Total Calcium: 131 mg.
Total Fiber: 2 gm.

Asparagus and Tomato Risotto

Serves 2
Prep time: 50 minutes

Stuffed Tomatoes with Lemon-Scented Couscous

Serves 2 to 3
Prep time: 15 minutes

An attractive, delicate pasta side dish that goes well with fish or poultry.

2 tomatoes
¾ cup water
¼ teaspoon grated lemon zest
1 teaspoon olive oil
½ cup couscous
3 tablespoons toasted pine nuts

1. Slice tomatoes in half, and remove and discard seeds and center portion of meat.
2. Toast pine nuts in oven at 350° for 5 minutes. Cool.
2. In a small saucepan, bring water to a boil. Stir in oil, couscous, and zest. Remove from heat and allow the mixture to stand covered for 5 minutes.
3. Fluff couscous with a fork and add pine nuts. Fill the hollowed tomato halves with mixture.

TOTAL CALORIES PER SERVING: 164

% Calories Carbohydrates: 32
% Calories Protein: 7
% Calories Fat: 62

Total Cholesterol: 0 mg.
Total Sodium: 16 mg.
Total Potassium: 316 mg.
Total Calcium: 13 mg.
Total Fiber: 4 gm.

A cold, crunchy grain salad with a distinctive, nutty flavor.

Dressing:
⅓ cup canola oil
⅓ cup white-wine vinegar or white-wine tarragon vinegar
4 tablespoons orange juice
2 teaspoons dried tarragon
½ teaspoon sea salt

Salad:
2 cups cooked kasha
¾ cup peas
¾ cup chopped carrots
1 small red bell pepper, diced
2 scallions, sliced
2 tablespoons fresh parsley, minced

1. Blend all dressing ingredients all and set aside.
2. In a large bowl, toss together kasha and vegetables until well combined.
3. Add dressing and toss again.
4. Serve with sliced oranges.

TOTAL CALORIES PER SERVING: 151

% Calories Carbohydrates: 25
% Calories Protein: 5
% Calories Fat: 69

Total Cholesterol: 0 mg.
Total Sodium: 69 mg.
Total Potassium: 455 mg.
Total Calcium: 60 mg.
Total Fiber: 2 gm.

Kasha Salad

Serves 3 to 4
Prep time: 20 minutes

Kashi Salad

Serves 2
Prep time: 10 minutes
(cooking time of kashi,
per package instructions)

Kashi combines oats, brown rice, whole rye, whole wheat, whole triticale, buckwheat, barley, and sesame seeds. It successfully combines complex carbohydrates, protein, and fiber into a single product—a fine addition to any athlete's diet.

2 cups kashi (found in most natural food stores)
3 tablespoons white-wine vinegar
3 tablespoons olive oil
1 teaspoon Dijon-style mustard
3 scallions, coarsely chopped
1 clove garlic
½ cup Italian parsley
ground pepper, to taste

1. Cook kashi according to package instructions. Set aside to cool.
2. Mix olive oil, vinegar, and mustard in bowl. Add kashi and combine well. Add scallions, garlic, and parsley. Season with pepper.

TOTAL CALORIES PER SERVING: 282

% Calories Carbohydrates: 22
% Calories Protein: 4
% Calories Fat: 75

Total Cholesterol: 0 mg.
Total Sodium: 47 mg.
Total Potassium: 450 mg.
Total Calcium: 90 mg.
Total Fiber: 10 gm.

This recipe is adapted from the *York Whole Food Restaurant Cookbook*. It is a vegetarian dish best served in the wintertime.

4 large potatoes
1 pound cooked lentils
2 medium onions
2 tablespoons canola oil
4 medium-sized carrots, grated or chopped
¼ pound mushrooms
2 teaspoons dried sage
2 tablespoons fresh parsley
1 12-ounce can of tomatoes, or 1 pound fresh tomatoes
4 tablespoons of low-fat or non-fat cheese (such as mozzarella)

1. Scrub potatoes until clean, and slice thinly lengthwise. Cook in boiling water, just until tender.
2. Cook lentils according to package instructions.
3. In a skillet, heat the oil and add onions, carrots, mushrooms and sage. When onions clear, and the carrots are tender, add tomatoes, and parsley. Season with just a little sea salt and fresh ground black pepper. Remove from the heat. Stir in the cooked lentils.
4. In a lightly greased 8 × 8 baking dish, put alternate layers of potato and the lentil mixture, starting and finishing with the potato. Top with cheese.
5. Bake at 350° for 30 minutes.

TOTAL CALORIES PER SERVING: 431

% Calories Carbohydrates: 62
% Calories Protein: 20
% Calories Fat: 18

Total Cholesterol: 5 mg.
Total Sodium: 184 mg.
Total Potassium: 1,691 mg.
Total Calcium: 267 mg.
Total Fiber: 11 gm.

Lentil and Potato Bake

Serves 4
Prep time: 25 minutes
Baking time: 30 minutes

Millet and Mushroom Bake

Serves 2
Prep time: 15 minutes
Cooking time: 20 minutes

An easily digested, mildly flavored grain dish. Try using exotic mushrooms such as shiitake, porcini, or chanterelle.

½ cup onion, minced
1 teaspoon butter or olive oil
⅓ cup dry white wine
1 cup fresh mushrooms, cleaned and sliced
½ cup peas, fresh or frozen
½ teaspoon dried sage
⅓ cup celery, minced
1 clove garlic, minced
2 cups millet, cooked

1. Preheat oven to 350°. Oil an 8- or 9-inch baking pan or glass casserole dish.
2. In a large skillet, over medium heat, saute onion in butter or olive oil and white wine for 5 minutes. Add mushrooms, celery, peas, and garlic. Cover, reduce heat, and cook for 10 minutes. Lift cover to stir occasionally.
3. Add millet and cook, stirring frequently. When millet is warm, spoon into baking pan. Bake 15 minutes, until top is lightly browned.

TOTAL CALORIES PER SERVING: 442

% Calories Carbohydrates: 76
% Calories Protein: 12
% Calories Fat: 12

Total Cholesterol: 0 mg.
Total Sodium: 45 mg.
Total Potassium: 1,643 mg.
Total Calcium: 117 mg.
Total Fiber: 3 gm.

A refreshing main dish salad. If you like, you can eliminate the chicken breast and prepare with cooked shrimp, or serve as a vegetarian entree.

Mediterranean Pasta Salad

Serves 4
Prep time: 35 minutes

Salad:
  1 chicken breast
  1 zucchini
  1 carrot, peeled
  1 cup peas (fresh or frozen)
  ¼ cup sun dried tomatoes (see note next page)
  ¼ cup sliced black olives
  ½ pound tri-color penne (or other thick-bodied pasta)
  pepper, garlic clove, rosemary, olive oil

---

1. Rub chicken breast with olive oil and peeled garlic clove. Sprinkle with ground black pepper and rosemary. Roast in a preheated 450° oven for 10 to 12 minutes; until the meat is no longer pink.
2. Cut carrots and zucchini into bite-size pieces. Lightly steam, along with peas, just until tender. Rinse vegetables with cold water to cool. Drain.
3. Cook pasta in a pot of hot boiling water with 1 teaspoon of oil and ½ teaspoon of salt until *al dente*. Cool.
4. Combine pasta and vegetables in a large bowl. Add chopped sun dried tomatoes and olives. Add dressing, toss, and serve.

Dressing:
  1 tablespoon fresh rosemary chopped up into tiny pieces (optional)
  1 teaspoon whole grain mustard
  ¼ cup olive oil
  2 tablespoons Balsamic vinegar

---

1. Allow rosemary to sit in olive oil while preparing pasta and vegetables (approx 30 minutes).
2. Combine herb scented oil with mustard and vinegar. Stir vigorously.

TOTAL CALORIES PER SERVING: 706

% Calories Carbohydrates: 57
% Calories Protein: 15
% Calories Fat: 28

Total Cholesterol: 18 mg.
Total Sodium: 180 mg.
Total Potassium: 406 mg.
Total Calcium: 65 mg.
Total Fiber: 2.5 gm.

SUN DRIED TOMATOES

Sun dried tomatoes can be purchased dried or packed in olive oil. When using the dry variety, allow the tomatoes to hydrate in water or oil for at least 30 minutes prior to use. In general, oil-packed sun dried tomatoes, purchased in jars from the gourmet section of your market, taste much better, and are recommended unless you are attempting to eat entirely fat-free.

Potato Ravioli can be served with any of the tomato pasta sauces found in **The Human Fuel Cookbook**, and makes a great pre-event carbo-load meal.

½ pound peeled red potatoes
2 cloves of garlic
1 tablespoon chopped fresh, or 1 teaspoon dried, parsley
¼ cup skim milk
1 teaspoon butter or olive oil
1 package Chinese wonton skins

1. Quarter and boil potatoes until very soft—about 20 minutes. Drain and set aside to cool.
2. Chop parsley with garlic.
3. When potatoes are cool, add garlic, parsley, milk, and butter. Mash until almost smooth.
4. Place about two teaspoons of potato mixture in the center of wonton skin. Moisten the edges with a little water and cover with the second skin. Press around the outside with your fingers in order to seal. Continue until all of the potato mixture is used.
5. Boil water in a large pot, and place 1 teaspoon of oil and a little salt in the water. Gently slide the ravioli into the water, and allow to cook until they float to the surface of the pot. This should take about 3 to 5 minutes.
6. Gently remove ravioli from water with a large, preferably slotted, spoon, and allow to drain.
7. Top with sauce.

TOTAL CALORIES PER SERVING: 291

% Calories Carbohydrates: 62
% Calories Protein: 9
% Calories Fat: 29

Total Cholesterol: 1 mg.
Total Sodium: 34 mg.
Total Potassium: 1,090 mg.
Total Calcium: 83 mg.
Total Fiber: 6 gm.

Potato Ravioli

Serves 2 to 3
Prep time: 1 hour

Additional Ravioli Fillings

Spinach and Ricotta Cheese

Here are three other tasty and healthful fillings for wonton skin ravioli....

Combine:

1 package chopped frozen spinach, drained
8-ounce package non-fat ricotta cheese
¼ teaspoon ground nutmeg

TOTAL CALORIES PER SERVING: 357

% Calories Carbohydrates: 17
% Calories Protein: 33
% Calories Fat: 50

Total Cholesterol: 76 mg.
Total Sodium: 354 mg.
Total Potassium: 624 mg.
Total Calcium: 731 mg.
Total Fiber: 0 gm.

Chicken and Ricotta Cheese

Combine:

1 boneless, skinless breast of cooked chicken, finely minced
1 8-ounce package non-fat ricotta cheese
3 tablespoons Italian parsley, minced

TOTAL CALORIES PER SERVING: 516

% Calories Carbohydrates: 15
% Calories Protein: 45
% Calories Fat: 40

Total Cholesterol: 149 mg.
Total Sodium: 405 mg.
Total Potassium: 971 mg.
Total Calcium: 803 mg.
Total Fiber: 0 gm.

Saute:

3 shallots, minced
1 clove garlic, minced
1 teaspoon olive oil

Combine with:

1 8- to 12-ounce package non-fat Ricotta cheese

TOTAL CALORIES PER SERVING: 486

% Calories Carbohydrates: 18
% Calories Protein: 40
% Calories Fat: 42

Total Cholesterol: 76 mg.
Total Sodium: 314 mg.
Total Potassium: 421 mg.
Total Calcium: 691 mg.
Total Fiber: 0 gm.

*Ricotta Cheese,
Shallots and Garlic*

Shepherd's Pie

Serves 2 to 3
Prep time: 1½ hours

This is a high-protein, high-carb vegetarian entree.

1 pound russet potatoes, peeled
4 ounces grated non-fat cheese
⅓ non-fat milk
1 tablespoon butter
8 ounces cooked brown lentils
1 12-ounces can tomatoes
½ pound carrots, sliced
½ pound parsnips, chopped coarsely
1 medium onion, chopped coarsely

1. Cook lentils with tomatoes and 2 cups water for about 45 minutes. Add carrots, parsnips, and onions, and boil for another 15 minutes.
2. Quarter the potatoes, and boil until tender. Mash them with milk and butter. Add grated cheese.
3. Place lentil mixture in the bottom of a lightly oiled square baking dish. Cover with the mashed potatoes. Bake in a pre-heated oven at 400° until the top is crispy, about 15 minutes.

TOTAL CALORIES PER SERVING: 757

% Calories Carbohydrates: 70
% Calories Protein: 20
% Calories Fat: 10

Total Cholesterol: 32 mg.
Total Sodium: 492 mg.
Total Potassium: 3,032 mg.
Total Calcium: 691 mg.
Total Fiber: 18 gm.

A delicious, hearty, and *foolproof* tomato meat sauce prepared with ground white meat poultry. Relatively low in fat, yet very satisfying.

4 teaspoons olive oil
1 medium onion, chopped
½ pound ground white meat chicken or turkey
¾ cup sliced freshmushrooms
4 cloves of garlic, peeled and chopped
1 28-ounce can chopped tomatoes
10 pitted black olives
sea salt and ground black pepper,
1 tablespoon dried, or 3 tablespoons fresh,
rosemary, minced
whole grain or artichoke spaghetti

Serves 2
Prep time: 45 minutes

1. Heat olive oil in large skillet. Add onions and saute until tender and transparent. Add ground chicken, mushrooms, and garlic. Continue until chicken is cooked, about 7 minutes. Season to taste. Add tomatoes and olives.
2. Reduce flame and cover pot. Simmer sauce, stirring occasionally, for 30 minutes.
3. While sauce is simmering, boil water, and cook whole grain or artichoke spaghetti according to package directions. Serve sauce over pasta. This dish is particularly good with freshly grated Parmesan, if your training can manage a "sodium splurge."

TOTAL CALORIES PER SERVING: 652

% Calories Carbohydrates: 27
% Calories Protein: 24
% Calories Fat: 48

Total Cholesterol: 87 mg.
Total Sodium: 500 mg.
Total Potassium: 1,091 mg.
Total Calcium: 97 mg.
Total Fiber: 4 gm.

Tabbouleh

A lemony, minty, cold grain salad made with bulgur wheat. Tabbouleh goes well with other Middle Eastern dishes, such as Hummus and Mediterranean vegetable salad.

Serves 3 to 4
Marinating time: 1 hour
Prep time: 20 minutes

1¼ cups bulgur wheat
1 cup + 1 tablespoon water
½ cup lemon juice
⅔ cup extra virgin olive oil
1 cup coarsely chopped fresh mint leaves
1 cup coarsely chopped fresh Italian parsley
1 teaspoon coarsely ground black pepper
2 teaspoons minced garlic
2 cups diced tomatoes (about 4 tomatoes)
1 cucumber, peeled and diced

1. Mix wheat, water, lemon juice, and olive oil in a large bowl. Set aside for about 30 minutes. Stir mixture occasionally.
2. Add mint, parsley, pepper, garlic, tomatoes, and cucumber. Stir mixture.
3. Chill for 30 or more minutes, then serve.

TOTAL CALORIES PER SERVING: 300

% Calories Carbohydrates: 31
% Calories Protein: 6
% Calories Fat: 63

Total Cholesterol: 0 mg.
Total Sodium: 282 mg.
Total Potassium: 533 mg.
Total Calcium: 99 mg.
Total Fiber: 3 gm.

5

FISH AND POULTRY

Baked Salmon with Dill

Serves 2
Prep time: 10 minutes
Baking time: 25 minutes

Dill is a classic complement to the flavor of salmon. Serve this dish with Cucumber Salad and Roasted Potatoes with Leeks for an easy-to-prepare, special occasion dinner!

¾ pound fresh salmon fillet
4 whole sprigs fresh dill
zest and juice of 1 lemon
1 large clove garlic, minced
olive oil
sea salt and freshly ground pepper to taste

1. Preheat oven to 350°.
2. Remove zest from lemon. Squeeze out juice.
3. Clean and dry salmon fillet, place in glass baking dish. Brush lightly with olive oil. Evenly sprinkle garlic, zest, and seasonings over fish. Arrange dill across the top. Add lemon juice.
4. Cover lightly with foil and bake for 15 minutes. Remove foil, and bake for an additional 10 minutes. Serve.

TOTAL CALORIES PER SERVING: 382

% Calories Carbohydrates: 5
% Calories Protein: 37
% Calories Fat: 59

Total Cholesterol: 112 mg.
Total Sodium: 273 mg.
Total Potassium: 742 mg.
Total Calcium: 69 mg.
Total Fiber: 0 gm.

SUCCESSFUL GRILLING TIPS

- To ensure even cooking, use a barbecue that closes and limit food thickness to $1\frac{1}{2}$ inches. Only food less than about $1\frac{1}{2}$ inches thick cooks evenly; thicker items will be overcooked on the outside by the time the inside is cooked.

- If you do not have a gas grill, prepare your barbecue 30 to 45 minutes prior to cooking. It takes that long for coals to get sufficiently hot. Coals are ready when they have a light layer of gray ash, under which you will be able to see a red-hot glow.

- Lightly brush grill with a non-saturated oil. This will prevent food from sticking.

- Consider using mesquite charcoal or mesquite wood chips as part of your fuel. Mesquite produces a distinctive, mild, woody aroma and taste.

- Protect your hands! Use long-handed tools and a fireproof mitt.

- After cooking, extinguish barbecue immediately. On an open grill, douse coals lightly with water. On a covered grill, cover the grill completely.

Barbecued Chicken with Lime-Tarragon Marinade

Serves 2 to 4
Marinating time: 1 hour
or more
Prep time: 15 minutes
Cooking time: 25 minutes

This dish makes a great centerpiece for a cold picnic lunch. Bring along some carrot salad and fresh baked whole grain bread. Remember that when cooking chicken pieces, white meat will cook faster than dark meat.

1 whole fryer chicken, split into eight pieces
¼ cup olive oil
juice of two limes
zest of 1 lime
¼ cup tarragon vinegar
2 sprigs of fresh tarragon, chopped, or 1 teaspoon dried
¼ cup white wine (optional)
sea salt and ground pepper to taste

1. Combine oil, lime, zest, vinegar, tarragon, wine, salt, and pepper in bowl with chicken.
2. Allow to marinate overnight.
3. Cook over medium hot coals or gas grill set on medium heat for 20 to 25 minutes with top of barbecue closed. Open frequently to turn and redistribute chicken, to ensure even cooking.

TOTAL CALORIES PER SERVING: 439

% Calories Carbohydrates: 8
% Calories Protein: 41
% Calories Fat: 51

Total Cholesterol: 133 mg.
Total Sodium: 220 mg.
Total Potassium: 374 mg.
Total Calcium: 40 mg.
Total Fiber: 0 gm.

Although a bottled dressing is recommended here for ease and speed, any of the homemade vinaigrette recipes provided in this book make a wonderful marinade for brochettes. You may also wish to try making brochettes with shrimp, or with a meaty fish like shark or swordfish.

2 medium bell peppers, seeded and cut into 1½-inch sections
1 large white onion, peeled and quartered
8 cherry tomatoes
1 pound chicken breast, cubed into 1-inch sections
4 12- to 16-inch wood skewers
bottled Italian dressing, or teriyaki sauce of your choice. (Take care to purchase a sauce or dressing made without sugar or artificial ingredients.)

1. In a shallow baking dish or bowl, marinate peppers, onions, tomatoes, and chicken in dressing for ½ hour or more. You can begin marinating up to 12 hours ahead of time. Keep chicken refrigerated while marinating.
2. Prepare grill.
3. Beginning with the pepper, alternately thread pieces of chicken, onion, tomatoes, and pepper onto skewers. Finish with a pepper. This will ensure that the ingredients do not slide off the skewer.
4. Grill for 8 to 10 minutes, turning sticks frequently. Cover barbecue when you are not turning.
5. Serve on a bed of brown rice or other grain.

TOTAL CALORIES PER SERVING: 593

% Calories Carbohydrates: 9
% Calories Protein: 12
% Calories Fat: 79

Total Cholesterol: 36 mg.
Total Sodium: 846 mg.
Total Potassium: 370 mg.
Total Calcium: 23 mg.
Total Fiber: 1.5 gm.

Chicken Brochette

Serves 4
Marinating time: 1 hour or more
Prep time: 20 to 30 minutes
Cooking time: 10 minutes

Chicken and Vegetable Rice Pilaf

Serves 2 to 3
Prep time: 30 minutes
Cooking time: 20 minutes

Don't be put off by the long list of ingredients. This is an easy, dependable, delicious meal in one dish.

1 whole chicken breast, carefully cleaned and cut into bite-size pieces
1 tablespoon olive oil
1 tablespoon butter
½ yellow onion, minced
1 red bell pepper, chopped
1 green bell pepper, chopped
1 cup mushrooms, stemmed and chopped
1 zucchini, chopped
⅓ cup scallions, chopped
½ teaspoon crushed, dried thyme
¼ teaspoon ground black pepper
¾ cup long grain brown rice
1 cup chicken stock or canned low-sodium chicken broth

1. Heat olive oil and butter in a large saucepan. Add onions and saute for 8 minutes. Add chicken, scallions, and mushrooms. Stir constantly for another 5 minutes.
2. Add seasonings, with zucchini and bell pepper. Stir.
3. Pour in rice, and saute for 1 additional minute. Pour in the chicken broth, stir for another 30 seconds, and cover. Cook on low flame for 20 minutes. Do not peek or stir during this time.
4. Open saucepan. Adjust seasonings as necessary, and serve in pasta bowls.

TOTAL CALORIES PER SERVING: 317

% Calories Carbohydrates: 21
% Calories Protein: 41
% Calories Fat: 37

Total Cholesterol: 79 mg.
Total Sodium: 596 mg.
Total Potassium: 549 mg.
Total Calcium: 42 mg.
Total Fiber: 1 gm.

Sea bass is a firm, mildly flavored fish. Be sure to purchase fish that is very fresh, without brown or bruised spots on it. Serve this dish with Spinach with Garlic and a simple grain dish.

1 pound fresh Chilean sea bass or, if unavailable,
red snapper
1 small yellow onion, chopped
1 shallot, minced
2 cloves garlic, minced
1 large tomato, chopped
¼ cup mixed fresh herbs (any two or more: basil,
tarragon, parsley, oregano)
½ cup white wine
sea salt and pepper to taste

1. Preheat oven to 375°.
2. Clean fish and pat dry with a paper towel. Place fish in a large ovenproof baking dish.
4. Sprinkle remainder of ingredients over top of fish. Cover loosely with foil.
5. Bake for 10 to 15 minutes, until fish is white and flaky.

TOTAL CALORIES PER SERVING: 289

% Calories Carbohydrates: 18
% Calories Protein: 64
% Calories Fat: 18

Total Cholesterol: 88 mg.
Total Sodium: 347 mg.
Total Potassium: 926 mg.
Total Calcium: 134 mg.
Total Fiber: 1 gm.

Chilean Sea Bass Provençal

Serves 2
Prep time: 15 minutes
Cooking time: 15 minutes

Ginger-Tamari Cornish Game Hens

Serves 2
Marinating time: 1 hour
or more
Prep time: 10 minutes
Cooking time: 1 hour

Serve this elegant, but easy-to-prepare, dish with wild rice and French String Beans à la Shields.

1 cup orange juice
3 tablespoons soy sauce
2 tablespoons fresh ginger, coarsely chopped
1 tablespoon honey
2 tablespoons canola oil
2 Cornish game hens, halved

1. Combine ingredients for the marinade thoroughly. Marinate game hens in ginger-tamari mixture for 1 or more hours. Refrigerate while marinating. You can leave the hens in the marinade overnight if it is more convenient, or for a slightly more intense flavor.
2. Pre-heat oven to 350°.
3. Bake hens in glass baking pan for 40 to 50 minutes or until done. Spoon juices from the bottom of the pan over the hens twice during baking to baste. A well baked hen will look white in color when sliced into, and the juices released will run clear. Be careful not to overcook.
4. Pour baking juices into a small saucepan. Cook over medium heat until liquid is reduced by half, about 5 minutes.
5. Pour sauce over each hen piece and serve.

TOTAL CALORIES PER SERVING: 355

% Calories Carbohydrates: 27
% Calories Protein: 26
% Calories Fat: 46

Total Cholesterol: 0 mg.
Total Sodium: 1,703 mg.
Total Potassium: 547 mg.
Total Calcium: 29 mg.
Total Fiber: 0 gm.

Rosemary, garlic, and lemon blend together to delicately accent the flavor of grilled chicken. Serve alongside a mixed green salad with a vinaigrette, Broccoli Andrew, and Broiled Potatoes.

1 whole chicken, 4 to 5 pounds.
¼ cup chopped + 1 whole sprig fresh, or
2 tablespoons + 1 teaspoon dried, rosemary
2 cloves garlic, peeled and halved
½ lemon
1 small yellow onion, peeled and quartered
sea salt and ground black pepper to taste

1. Clean and pat chicken with a paper towel to remove excess moisture.
2. Rub skin of chicken with halved garlic clove and lemon half.
3. Sprinkle with sea salt and pepper.
4. Slightly loosen skin of chicken from meat. Put rosemary into the gaps between skin and meat.
5. Place onion, lemon half, and garlic into the empty cavity of chicken. Place one sprig, or 1 teaspoon dried, rosemary inside as well.
6. On barbecue, place a small, lightweight foil pie tin under the grill to catch fat as it drips from the chicken. Make sure that charcoal is on each side of the drip pan but not directly underneath. This way of barbecuing is often referred to as the "indirect method." Cook covered, 20 minutes per pound of meat.

TOTAL CALORIES PER SERVING: 393

% Calories Carbohydrates: 7
% Calories Protein: 45
% Calories Fat: 48

Total Cholesterol: 133 mg.
Total Sodium: 219 mg.
Total Potassium: 368 mg.
Total Calcium: 40 mg.
Total Fiber: 0 gm.

Grilled Rosemary Chicken

Makes 1 whole chicken
Serves 2 to 4
Prep time: 15 minutes
Cooking time: 1 hour, 15 minutes

Grilled Whole Trout

Serves 2
Prep time: 15 minutes
Cooking time: 10 minutes

Trout is a fresh water, delicately flavored fish. It is well complemented by the aromatic tang of fresh herbs and citrus. Because the flesh is so fragile, it is best to prepare the fish with the skin on, remove just before serving.

2 fresh whole trout, boned, but with head and tail still on
olive oil
1 lemon, thinly sliced
1 bunch arugala or rosemary
2 tablespoons bread crumbs
1 clove garlic, halved
sea salt and freshly ground black pepper to taste

1. Lightly brush outside of trout with olive oil. This will prevent the fish from sticking to the grill. Rub inside of trout with garlic half.
2. Place 2 to 3 lemon slices inside the trout. Place herbs on top. Sprinkle with bread crumbs. Use string or wood toothpicks to hold fish closed.
3. Place on grill or in broiler. Allow to cook for five minutes on each side. The flesh of the trout should be white.

TOTAL CALORIES PER SERVING: 145

% Calories Carbohydrates: 26
% Calories Protein: 52
% Calories Fat: 22

Total Cholesterol: 48 mg.
Total Sodium: 291 mg.
Total Potassium: 524 mg.
Total Calcium: 72 mg.
Total Fiber: 0 gm.

This dish has a flavorful citrus sauce that contains absolutely no fat! It is delicious with any steamed whole grain, and goes well with snow peas and carrots.

1 large chicken breast, split into halves
½ Valencia orange, thinly sliced
½ cup orange juice
2 tablespoons white-wine vinegar
2 small shallots, chopped
1 tablespoon orange zest (optional)

1. Place well-cleaned chicken in a shallow pan with juice from ½ orange, orange juice, vinegar, shallots, and zest. Allow to marinate for 1 hour or more, redistributing marinade every now and again.
2. Cook chicken on a gas grill on medium, or over medium-hot coals. Grill covered, skin side down, for 10 minutes. Turn, and cook for another 10 minutes, or until meat is no longer pink and juices run clear.

TOTAL CALORIES PER SERVING: 206

% Calories Carbohydrates: 30
% Calories Protein: 57
% Calories Fat: 14

Total Cholesterol: 73 mg.
Total Sodium: 62 mg.
Total Potassium: 441 mg.
Total Calcium: 41 mg.
Total Fiber: 0 gm.

Chicken Breasts à l'Orange

Serves 2
Marinating time: 1 hour or more
Prep time: 10 minutes
Cooking time 20 minutes

Liane's
Roast Turkey

Makes 1 medium turkey
Serves 10 to 12
Prep time: 45 minutes to
1 hour
Cooking time: 4½ to 5
hours

This is a basic recipe for preparing a holiday turkey. It can be stuffed with wild rice cooked with chopped celery and onions, or prepared more simply with a quartered apple and an additional quartered onion inside the cavities of the turkey for flavor.

For a lower-fat alternative, you can purchase just the turkey breast. To ensure tenderness, cover the bottom of the pan with one inch of water or chicken broth. Baking time for a breast will be between 1½ to 2 hours.

1 16- to 18-pound turkey
1 large onion
¼ cup sweet butter, or ⅓ cup vegetable oil
4 cloves garlic
paprika
sage
sea salt
pepper

1. Wash out the two cavities of the turkey, and dry with a paper towel. Rub half the chopped garlic cloves into both cavities. It's best to actually sew the cavities closed with needle and thread, making 1-inch stitches.
2. Chop onion into six pieces. Scatter them in the bottom of a roasting or other large baking pan. Melt butter or add oil to the remaining garlic over a low heat. Add pepper and ¼ teaspoon sea salt. Rub mixture all over the turkey. Put in baking/roasting pan with the breast side up.
3. Place in a 325° oven, with a piece of foil tented lightly over the top of the turkey breast.
4. After 1½ hours, begin to baste (brush) the turkey with the juices gathered on the bottom of the pan every 20 minutes. Remove foil for the last hour. A 16-pound stuffed turkey is done in 4½ to 5 hours. An un-stuffed turkey takes about ½ hour less. You can tell a turkey is done if you can move drumsticks around easily and if, when cut into, juices run clear. You can also purchase a turkey with a sensor that pops out when the turkey is done. Be sure not to overcook turkey. It will continue to cook after it is removed from oven, from its own retained heat.

TOTAL CALORIES PER SERVING: 862

% Calories Carbohydrates: 1
% Calories Protein: 77
% Calories Fat: 22

Total Cholesterol: 280 mg.
Total Sodium: 78 mg.
Total Potassium: 26 mg.
Total Calcium: 8 mg.
Total Fiber: 0 gm.

Whitefish Baked in Foil

Serves 2
Prep time: 15 minutes
Cooking time: 10 to 12
minutes

Fish that has lived in clean waters is healthful, easily digestible, and quite delicious. Baking fish in wrapped packages intensifies aroma and flavor. Serve with Asparagus Dijonaise, grilled tomatoes, and Millet and Mushroom Bake.

2 6-ounce whitefish fillets
2 tablespoons fresh lemon juice
4 slices fresh lemon, seeded
2 cloves garlic, minced
2 sprigs fresh, or 2 teaspoons dried, tarragon
2 pieces of foil (or parchment paper), approx 12 x 10
sea salt and freshly ground black pepper to taste

1. Preheat oven to 400°.
2. Rinse and dry fish. Place each fillet in the center of a foil square. Sprinkle lemon juice on fillets. Follow with garlic, lemon slices, and tarragon.
3. Seal foil packets. Place in a baking pan or a sheet with sides. Bake for 10 to 12 minutes. You can serve the fish right in the foil packet, or remove and place on a warm plate (fish gets cold very quickly).

TOTAL CALORIES PER SERVING: 246

% Calories Carbohydrates: 5
% Calories Protein: 56
% Calories Fat: 39

Total Cholesterol: 102 mg.
Total Sodium: 280 mg.
Total Potassium: 621 mg.
Total Calcium: 30 mg.
Total Fiber: 0 gm.

6

BREADS AND MUFFINS

TIPS FOR MAKING GREAT MUFFINS AND QUICK BREADS...

- Be sure to preheat. Preheating your oven to 400° 15 minutes prior to baking will ensure proper rising.

- Do not overmix batter. Gently and briefly stir wet and dry ingredients together. It's okay if the batter is a little lumpy. Proper mixing will create muffins that have a light, chewy consistency.

- Slightly grease the tins for easy removal.

- Fill unused muffin cups half-way with water. This will prevent scorching, and keep other muffins moist.

- Do not overbake. Muffins should bake in 20 to 25 minutes. When done, they will be lightly brown on top, springy to the touch, and a toothpick inserted into the center will come out clean.

THE USE OF EGGS IN BAKING

In any of the recipes for baked goods in this book, you may substitute 2 egg whites for 1 whole egg. This will eliminate cholesterol and reduce the fat and calorie content. Since the fat in egg yolks acts as a shortening and adds color, you can expect that baked goods prepared with egg whites only will be somewhat drier and lighter in color.

These fiber-packed, easy-to-prepare muffins are a great alternative to a plain bowl of cereal for breakfast.

1¼ cups oat bran
½ cup unbleached flour
¾ cup whole wheat pastry flour
2 teaspoons baking powder
¼ teaspoon sea salt
1 cup non-fat milk
½ cup + 1 tablespoon honey
2 egg whites
¼ cup canola oil
1 cup blueberries

1. Preheat the oven to 375°.
2. Mix oat bran, flour, baking powder, and salt in a large bowl.
3. Mix together milk, honey, and egg whites.
4. Pour wet ingredients over dry ingredients, and fold the two together with a fork or rubber spatula using as few strokes as possible to mix. Fold in blueberries.
5. Spoon batter onto prepared muffin cups. Bake for 20 minutes, until firm and lightly browned.

TOTAL CALORIES PER SERVING: 220

% Calories Carbohydrates: 58
% Calories Protein: 14
% Calories Fat: 28

Total Cholesterol: 1 mg.
Total Sodium: 102 mg.
Total Potassium: 235 mg.
Total Calcium: 100 mg.
Total Fiber: 3 gm.

Blueberry Oat Bran Muffins

Makes 12 muffins
Prep time: 15 minutes
Baking time: 20 minutes

Corn Bread

Serves 4
Prep time: 10 minutes
Baking time: 10 minutes

The use of coarsely ground cornmeal will give the crust of this cornbread a crispier consistency. To produce a sweet corn bread, add 2 tablespoons of honey to the batter and brush the top crust with a third.

1 cup yellow cornmeal
½ teaspoon sea salt
½ teaspoon baking soda
1 cup buttermilk (or skim milk, for less tangy results)
1 egg
⅓ cup corn (fresh or frozen)
2 teaspoons extra virgin olive oil

1. Preheat oven to 450°. Grease a 9-inch square baking pan with olive oil. Put pan in oven to warm for five minutes.
2. Combine cornmeal, salt and baking soda in a large bowl. In a small bowl, mix buttermilk and egg until combined.
3. Pour liquid mixture into dry ingredients. Add corn. Stir until just combined. Be careful not to overmix the batter.
4. Put batter in warmed pan. Bake for 10 minutes, or until bread is firm and a toothpick or knife inserted into the center comes out clean.

TOTAL CALORIES PER SERVING: 222

% Calories Carbohydrates: 49
% Calories Protein: 12
% Calories Fat: 39

Total Cholesterol: 71 mg.
Total Sodium: 184 mg.
Total Potassium: 202 mg.
Total Calcium: 114 mg.
Total Fiber: 1 gm.

These muffins are a wonderful complement to a traditional Thanksgiving meal.

2 navel oranges
1½ cups whole wheat pastry flour
½ cup unbleached flour
1 tablespoon baking powder
½ cup apple juice concentrate
¼ cup plus 3 tablespoons chopped dates
¼ cup canola oil
2 egg whites
1 cup cranberries, coarsely chopped
1 cup walnuts, chopped

1. Preheat oven to 400°. Lightly grease 12 muffin cups, or set out 12 paper muffin cups.
2. Remove zest from one orange and chop finely. Extract juice from oranges. Set aside ⅔ cup orange juice.
3. In blender, combine oil, apple juice concentrate, and dates. In a medium bowl, add this mixture to ⅔ cup orange juice and egg. Mix until blended.
4. In another bowl, toss together cranberries, nuts, and orange zest. In a third bowl, mix flour and baking powder.
5. Pour liquid over flour mixture and combine. Add the cranberry and nut mixture, and distribute evenly.
6. Evenly divide batter into 12 muffin cups. Bake for 20 to 25 minutes.
7. Remove from oven, and allow muffins to sit for two minutes before removing from pan. Cool for 15 minutes prior to serving.

TOTAL CALORIES PER SERVING: 260

% Calories Carbohydrates: 38
% Calories Protein: 11
% Calories Fat: 51

Total Cholesterol: 0 mg.
Total Sodium: 37 mg.
Total Potassium: 265 mg.
Total Calcium: 59 mg.
Total Fiber: 0 gm.

Cranberry-Orange Walnut Muffins

Makes 12 muffins
Prep time:
15 to 20 minutes
Baking Time: 25 minutes

Maple Walnut
Quick Bread

Makes 1 loaf
Prep time: 15 minutes
Baking time: 50 minutes

Be sure to use 100% pure maple syrup (the pure sap of maple trees, reduced by boiling), rather than the processed maple flavored syrups frequently found in markets. The later are flavored artificially and sweetened with corn syrup.

1½ cups whole wheat pastry flour
½ cup unbleached flour
1 teaspoon baking soda
1 teaspoon baking powder
½ teaspoon salt
½ cup canola oil
½ cup maple syrup
4 egg whites
1 cup non-fat vanilla or maple flavored yogurt
1 teaspoon vanilla
1 cup walnuts, coarsely chopped

1. Preheat oven to 350°. Lightly grease a loaf pan with canola oil.
2. In a large bowl, use a fork to combine flours, baking powder, baking soda, and salt.
3. In a medium bowl, combine canola oil, maple syrup, and eggs. Beat until creamy. Add yogurt and vanilla and stir for 2 more minutes.
4. Pour wet ingredients into flour mixture. Stir until just combined. Fold in walnuts.
5. Pour batter into prepared loaf pan. Bake for 45 to 50 minutes. Allow to cool 15 to 20 minutes before removing from pan. While bread is still warm, brush top with maple syrup.

TOTAL CALORIES PER SERVING: 295

% Calories Carbohydrates: 28
% Calories Protein: 12
% Calories Fat: 60

Total Cholesterol: 2 mg.
Total Sodium: 87 mg.
Total Potassium: 216 mg.
Total Calcium: 77 mg.
Total Fiber: 0 gm.

During the summer months, these muffins can be prepared with fresh peaches. Use very ripe, soft peaches, and be sure to peel them first.

2 cups whole wheat pastry flour
½ cup unbleached flour
1 tablespoon baking powder
¼ teaspoon salt
¼ cup vegetable oil
½ cup + 1 tablespoon honey
1 egg
1 cup non-fat milk
1 16-ounce can peaches, packed in their own juice
(no sugar added), well drained and coarsely
chopped
2 tablespoons poppy seeds

1. Preheat oven to 400°. Lightly grease 12 muffin cups, or set out paper muffin cups.
2. Combine flour, baking powder, and salt in a medium bowl.
3. In a second bowl, combine oil, honey, egg, and milk.
4. Pour liquid over dry ingredients, stir only until combined. Fold in peaches and poppy seeds.
5. Evenly divide into 12 muffin cups, and bake for 20 to 25 minutes, until golden brown. Serve while still warm.

TOTAL CALORIES PER SERVING: 164

% Calories Carbohydrates: 61
% Calories Protein: 11
% Calories Fat: 28

Total Cholesterol: 1 mg.
Total Sodium: 66 mg.
Total Potassium: 170 mg.
Total Calcium: 76 mg.
Total Fiber: 0 gm.

Peach Poppy Seed Muffins

Makes 12 muffins
Prep time: 15 minutes
Baking time: 25 minutes

Whole Wheat Bread

Makes 1 loaf
Prep time: 1 hour, over a
3-hour period
Baking time: 20 to 40
minutes

The aroma of fresh bread baking in your own kitchen will convince you that homemade bread is well worth the time and effort.

2 cups non-fat milk
3 tablespoons oil
1½ teaspoons salt
3 tablespoons fruit juice concentrate
2 packages dry yeast
⅓ cup lukewarm water
¾ cup unbleached white flour
5 to 6 cups whole wheat bread flour

1. Heat milk to almost boiling (scalding). Add oil, salt, and juice concentrate. Remove from heat to large bowl, and allow to cool until lukewarm.
2. Dissolve yeast in lukewarm water. Stir once or twice, using a wooden spoon. Add to other liquid ingredients.
3. Add the white flour and two cups of the whole wheat flour, and stir until you have a smooth, thick batter. Add 2½ cups more flour and begin to combine, using your hands.
4. Turn dough out onto a floured surface, and knead. Add more flour as needed to keep dough from becoming sticky. Knead dough until it is smooth and elastic—about 10 minutes.
5. Grease a bowl lightly with oil. Put dough in bowl and cover with a slightly damp cloth or towel. Allow dough to rise in a warm place until it doubles in bulk—about 1 hour.
6. Flatten, or "punch down," dough. Cover again, and allow it to rise for another hour.
7. Knead for 1 to 2 minutes, and shape dough into fist-sized rolls or two loaves. Place them in greased baking pans. Cover, and let rise again for 35 to 45 minutes, until they have doubled in size.
8. Preheat oven to 375°. Bake rolls for 20 to 25 minutes; bake loaves of bread for 40 minutes. Bread is done when the top is brown and crisp, and it makes a hollow sound when you tap on it.

Bread making is tricky! Practice is the key here. Don't get discouraged if your first attempt does not result in perfect loaves. Even early efforts make for good eating.

TOTAL CALORIES PER SERVING: 281

% Calories Carbohydrates: 70　　Total Cholesterol: 2 mg.
% Calories Protein: 15　　Total Sodium: 76 mg.
% Calories Fat: 15　　Total Potassium: 337 mg.
Total Calcium: 97 mg.
Total Fiber: 0 gm.

7

BREAKFAST

Blueberry Corn Pancakes

Serves 2 to 3
Prep time: 15 minutes
Cooking time: 10 minutes

When blueberries are out of season, prepare these pancakes with strawberries, bananas, or raisins.

½ cup whole wheat pastry flour
½ cup cornmeal
½ teaspoon baking soda
2 large egg whites
1 cup skim milk
1 tablespoon unsweetened apple juice concentrate or honey
1 tablespoon vanilla
1 tablespoon canola oil, or non-stick spray
1 cup blueberries

1. Sift flour and cornmeal together with baking soda.
2. Add eggs, milk, juice or honey, and vanilla, and stir until just combined.
3. Heat oil in non-stick skillet over medium heat.
4. Use ¼-cup measure to spoon batter onto skillet. Sprinkle with blueberries. Turn pancakes when bubbles begin to appear and edges begin to dry. Cook other side until golden brown.

TOTAL CALORIES PER SERVING: 378

% Calories Carbohydrates: 64
% Calories Protein: 15
% Calories Fat: 21

Total Cholesterol: 2 mg.
Total Sodium: 226 mg.
Total Potassium: 518 mg.
Total Calcium: 238 mg.
Total Fiber: 2 gm.

An impressive, surprisingly easy-to-make Sunday breakfast treat. Serve flat or rolled up with fresh apple-sauce (p. 116) or maple syrup.

¾ cup whole wheat pastry flour
¼ teaspoon baking powder
2 teaspoons apple juice concentrate
1⅓ cup non-fat milk (or, for a tangier flavor, use low-fat buttermilk)
2 egg whites
½ teaspoon vanilla
½ teaspoon cinnamon

1. Lightly grease griddle or non-stick fry pan.
2. Mix together flour and baking powder in a large bowl.
3. Add all remaining ingredients.
4. Pour ¼ cup of batter at a time into hot pan. Allow to cook until the top of the crêpe is bubbly. Gently flip crêpe. Grill for 1 to 2 more minutes.
5. Store crêpes in a warm (250°) oven until all crêpes are prepared and you are ready to serve.

TOTAL CALORIES PER SERVING: 311

% Calories Carbohydrates: 76
% Calories Protein: 21
% Calories Fat: 4

Total Cholesterol: 7 mg.
Total Sodium: 203 mg.
Total Potassium: 581 mg.
Total Calcium: 314 mg.
Total Fiber: 0 gm.

Breakfast Crêpes

Serves 2
Prep time: 10 minutes
Cooking time: 20 minutes

Egg White Omelettes

Serves 2
Prep time: 10 minutes
Cooking time: 15 minutes

The basic omelette can be filled with any combination of sauteed or steamed vegetables. Described here is a basic mushroom and cheese filling.

8 egg whites
¼ cup non-fat milk
¼ teaspoon sea salt
⅛ teaspoon ground black pepper
2 teaspoons unsalted butter
1 cup fresh mushrooms, cleaned and sliced
½ yellow onion, finely chopped
1 ounce non-fat cheese, thinly sliced or grated

1. Combine egg whites, milk, salt, and pepper in blender.
2. Melt butter in a small non-stick pan. Saute mushrooms and onion until mushrooms are tender and onions are translucent. This will take 3 to 5 minutes. Remove from heat, and place in medium bowl. Cover loosely with foil to keep warm.
3. Blend egg mixture on high until light and frothy—about 2 minutes.
4. Heat pan again. Add half of the egg mixture, and cook over a medium heat until the bottom is lightly browned and the top is set but still moist.
5. Place half of the mushroom mixture and cheese on one side of the omelette. Fold over and slide onto plate.
6. Repeat steps 4 and 5 for second omelette.

TOTAL CALORIES PER SERVING: 170

% Calories Carbohydrates: 23
% Calories Protein: 50
% Calories Fat: 27

Total Cholesterol: 15 mg.
Total Sodium: 334 mg.
Total Potassium: 311 mg.
Total Calcium: 160 mg.
Total Fiber: 0 gm.

Fruity Breakfast Muesli

Serves 2
Prep time: 15 minutes
Baking time: 5 minutes

Serve with skim milk or non-fat yogurt of any flavor.

¾ cup rolled oats
½ cup slivered almonds
4 tablespoons maple sugar (purchase at your local health food store)
½ teaspoon ground cinnamon
½ apple, cored and diced
½ cup currants or raisins
1 sliced banana, or ½ cup fresh berries in season, or both!

1. Pre-heat oven to 375°. Place oats and almonds in the bottom of a shallow pan or cookie sheet. Sprinkle maple sugar and cinnamon on top. Toast in oven for 5 to 7 minutes, until oats are crispy and almonds are light brown in color. Allow to cool. (This mixture can be prepared ahead and stored in an airtight container).
2. Add to fruit, and stir to combine. Serve immediately.

TOTAL CALORIES PER SERVING: 925

% Calories Carbohydrates: 52
% Calories Protein: 12
% Calories Fat: 36

Total Cholesterol: 0 mg.
Total Sodium: 16 mg.
Total Potassium: 1,501 mg.
Total Calcium: 270 mg.
Total Fiber: 15 gm.

Health for Life Granola

Makes 6 cups
Prep time: 30 minutes
Cooking time: 30 minutes

Granola is a sweet and crunchy breakfast or snack food that's high in carbs and calories—perfect for a pre-event treat. Make ahead and store in an airtight container for convenience.

3½ cups rolled oats
½ cup raw, unsalted sunflower seeds
½ cup sliced raw almonds
¼ cup raw pecans
¼ cup sesame seeds
¼ cup honey
¼ cup canola oil
⅛ to ¼ cup water (as needed to moisten)
½ cup raisins or currants
½ cup dates, dried cherries, or dried apples (or any combination of the three), chopped

1. Preheat oven to 325°.
2. Combine all ingredients except raisins and dried fruit in a large bowl. Stir. Add just enough water to moisten.
3. Pour ingredients onto a large cookie sheet. Bake for 30 minutes, or until golden brown. Allow to cool for 15 minutes.
4. Stir in dried fruit. Store in an airtight container or jar.

TOTAL CALORIES PER SERVING: 334

% Calories Carbohydrates: 14
% Calories Protein: 43
% Calories Fat: 43

Total Cholesterol: 0 mg.
Total Sodium: 4 mg.
Total Potassium: 422 mg.
Total Calcium: 62 mg.
Total Fiber: 6 gm.

The classic breakfast cereal revisited—there's nothing like the warmth and comfort of oatmeal on a cold winter morning.

⅔ cup rolled oats
1½ cups water
1 teaspoon vanilla
⅓ cup raisins
½ teaspoon cinnamon
1 banana, sliced

1. Combine all ingredients except banana in a medium saucepan. Bring to boil.
2. Cover pot and lower heat. Simmer for 4 to 5 minutes. Stir occasionally.
3. For a creamier consistency, let stand covered for 5 more minutes.
4. Divide into two bowls, and top with banana slices. Serve with non-fat milk, toasted walnuts, and honey, as desired.

TOTAL CALORIES PER SERVING: 181

% Calories Carbohydrates: 86
% Calories Protein: 7
% Calories Fat: 7

Total Cholesterol: 0 mg.
Total Sodium: 147 mg.
Total Potassium: 466 mg.
Total Calcium: 104 mg.
Total Fiber: 4 gm.

Old-Fashioned Oatmeal

Serves 2
Prep time: 5 minutes
Cooking time: 5 minutes

Orange-Scented Waffles

Serves 2
Prep time: 15 minutes
Cooking time: 15 minutes

Crispy on the outside, soft and chewy on the inside, waffles are delicious and remarkably easy to make. Borrow a waffle iron from a friend, or purchase your own from your local department store.

2 large egg whites
½ cup non-fat milk
½ cup non-fat vanilla yogurt
2 tablespoons orange juice
1 tablespoon orange zest, grated
1 cup whole wheat pastry flour
1 teaspoon baking powder
½ teaspoon baking soda
⅓ cup raisins

1. Preheat waffle iron and spray with non-stick spray.
2. Combine egg whites, milk, yogurt, juice, and zest in a medium bowl. Mix vigorously with a whisk.
3. Combine dry ingredients. Add liquids and mix until just combined. Fold in raisins.
4. Use ½-cup measure to pour batter into the center of waffle iron. Cook until golden brown, approximately 5 to 7 minutes, depending upon the waffle iron. Serve topped with fresh orange sections and orange or other flavored non-fat yogurt, or with maple syrup.

TOTAL CALORIES PER SERVING: 634

% Calories Carbohydrates: 68
% Calories Protein: 26
% Calories Fat: 6

Total Cholesterol: 32 mg.
Total Sodium: 758 mg.
Total Potassium: 1,690 mg.
Total Calcium: 1,165 mg.
Total Fiber: 2 gm.

8

SANDWICHES

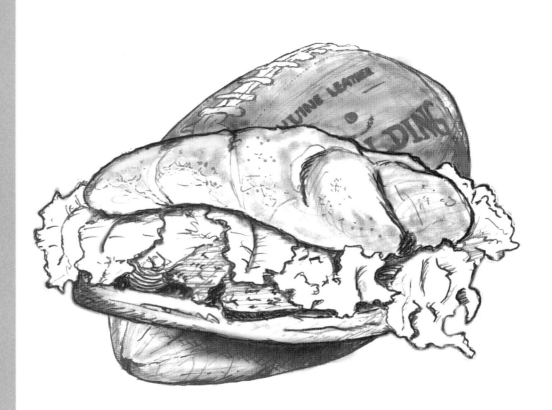

Easy Pizza

Serves 2
Prep time: 5 minutes
Cooking time: 10 minutes
Prep time for dough:
1½ hours

Most health food stores carry a prepared, whole-grain flat pizza bread. It is usually found in the bread section. You may also use a prepared frozen dough, or, if you feel enthusiastic enough, you can make your own from scratch.

Pizza Dough (makes enough for 1 large or 2 small pizzas):
1 cup very warm water
1 package active dry yeast
1½ cup whole wheat flour
1 cup unbleached flour
2 tablespoons olive oil
¼ teaspoon salt

1. Dissolve yeast in warm water. Add flour, a little at a time, and then add oil and salt. Using your hands, form the dough into a ball.
2. Place the dough on a lightly floured surface. Knead dough until it is smooth and elastic. This will take between 5 and 7 minutes. If the dough gets sticky again, add a little more flour.
3. Place dough in a lightly oiled bowl. Cover the bowl with a damp kitchen towel, and allow the dough to rise in a warm place for 1 hour.
4. Divide the dough into two parts. Roll into round disks. Cover them and let rise for another 15 minutes. Roll out dough into two 12-inch pizza crusts.
(Or use 1 large-size "Boboli" or other prepared pizza bread

Pizza Topping:
1 cup low-fat grated mozzarella or non-dairy soya cheese
3 Italian plum tomatoes, sliced and quartered
1 cup mixed vegetables (such as spinach, mushrooms, broccoli, or zucchini)

1. Preheat oven to 450°.
2. Cover pizza dough or bread with tomatoes.
Sprinkle with chopped mixed vegetables, and then
cheese.
3. Heat in oven until cheese bubbles and starts to
brown. Slice and serve.

TOTAL CALORIES PER SERVING: 483

% Calories Carbohydrates: 46
% Calories Protein: 21
% Calories Fat: 33

Total Cholesterol: 30 mg.
Total Sodium: 332 mg.
Total Potassium: 436 mg.
Total Calcium: 497 mg.
Total Fiber: 0 gm.

Bruschetta

Serves 2
Prep time: 15 minutes

Bruschetta is a delicious Tuscan open-faced sandwich.

3 ripe, Italian plum tomatoes, cut into small bite-size chunks
4 to 6 basil leaves, sliced into thin strips
1 shallot, minced
1 clove garlic, minced
1 tablespoon red-wine vinegar
2 tablespoons olive oil
freshly ground pepper
2 large, thick slices of sourdough bread

Combine ingredients and spoon on top of toasted bread brushed with olive oil. Serve at room temperature.

TOTAL CALORIES PER SERVING: 222

% Calories Carbohydrates: 34
% Calories Protein: 8
% Calories Fat: 58

Total Cholesterol: 0 mg.
Total Sodium: 146 mg.
Total Potassium: 307 mg.
Total Calcium: 103 mg.
Total Fiber: 1 gm.

A crunchy, more healthful approach to an old favorite.

1 6-ounce can white meat tuna packed in water, rinsed
2 small or 1 large carrot, minced fine
1 celery stalk, minced fine
½ onion, minced
¼ cup lemon juice
½ teaspoon freshly ground pepper.

1. Mash tuna with a fork until it is the consistency you prefer.
2. Add the rest of the ingredients and mix thoroughly.
3. Divide into two servings. Serve on any whole grain bread, with alfalfa sprouts and tomato slices, if you like.

TOTAL CALORIES PER SERVING: 209

% Calories Carbohydrates: 36
% Calories Protein: 56
% Calories Fat: 8

Total Cholesterol: 0 mg.
Total Sodium: 485 mg.
Total Potassium: 553 mg.
Total Calcium: 35 mg.
Total Fiber: 3 gm.

Fat-Free Tuna Fish Salad Sandwiches

Serves 2
Prep time: 15 minutes

Hummus and Mediterranean Vegetable Salad Sandwiches

Serves 4
Prep time: 25 minutes

Hummus can also be served as a vegetable dip, while the Mediterranean Vegetable Salad also works well as a starter or side dish.

pita bread (available in whole grain variety in all health food stores, and some markets)

Hummus:
1 15-ounce can garbanzo beans (chick-peas)
⅓ cup hot water
5 tablespoons lemon juice (approximately the juice of one large lemon)
2 large cloves garlic, finely minced
¼ cup tahini (sesame seed paste)

Vegetable Salad:
1 cucumber, peeled
1 large tomato
2 carrots, peeled
1 green pepper
juice of one medium lemon
2 tablespoons olive oil
sea salt and ground black pepper to taste

1. Chop vegetables into small bite-size pieces. Place in bowl with lemon juice, olive oil, and seasoning. Place in fridge to marinate.
2. Grind up garbanzo beans with hot water in food processor or blender until it forms a smooth paste. Add lemon juice, garlic, and tahini, and stir.
3. Stuff a dollop of hummus and a few heaping tablespoons of vegetable salad into warm pita bread halves, and serve.

TOTAL CALORIES PER SERVING: 341

% Calories Carbohydrates: 49
% Calories Protein: 14
% Calories Fat: 37

Total Cholesterol: 0 mg.
Total Sodium: 247 mg.
Total Potassium: 648 mg.
Total Calcium: 93 mg.
Total Fiber: 4 gm.

Quesadillas are an easy-to-prepare, hot tortilla sandwich. This is our version of the traditional Mexican dish, usually made with high-fat cheese, tortillas prepared with lard, and sour cream. Serve with our Easy Tomato Salsa on page 136.

whole wheat or corn tortillas
non-fat cheddar cheese
avocado
cilantro, yogurt, and salsa for garnish (optional)

1. Lay a tortilla on a non-stick skillet over medium heat. While tortilla is heating, place thinly sliced or grated cheese on the top. Add slices of avocado. As cheese begins to melt, place a second tortilla on top, and flip.
2. Remove from heat and slice into halves or quarters. Serve with cilantro, salsa, and non-fat plain yogurt.

TOTAL CALORIES PER SERVING: 547

% Calories Carbohydrates: 57
% Calories Protein: 10
% Calories Fat: 33

Total Cholesterol: 2 mg.
Total Sodium: 950 mg.
Total Potassium: 2,152 mg.
Total Calcium: 265 mg.
Total Fiber: 7 gm.

Quesadillas

Serves 2
Prep time: 10 minutes
Cooking time: 5 minutes

Turkey Burgers

Serves 2
Prep time: 10 minutes
Cooking time: 15 minutes

Here's a guilt-free way to satisfy your burger craving with low-fat, high-protein, turkey meat.

½ pound ground turkey breast
1 egg white
1 tablespoon Dijon mustard
½ small yellow onion, minced
sea salt and ground black pepper to taste

1. In a medium bowl, combine ingredients well.
2. Form into 2 patties, and broil or grill on barbecue. Cooking time should be about 15 minutes.
3. Serve on whole grain buns and garnish with any combination of lettuce, tomato slices, sprouts, avocado, and sliced sweet red onions.

TOTAL CALORIES PER SERVING: 312

% Calories Carbohydrates: 32
% Calories Protein: 33
% Calories Fat: 35

Total Cholesterol: 90 mg.
Total Sodium: 550 mg.
Total Potassium: 170 mg.
Total Calcium: 15 mg.
Total Fiber: 3 gm.

9

DESSERTS

Baked Apples

Serves 2
Prep time: 10 minutes
Baking time: 45 minutes

A sweet, warm, comforting dessert that is easy to make.

2 large Golden Delicious apples
2 tablespoons walnuts, finely chopped
2 tablespoons currants or raisins
2 tablespoons dates, finely chopped
1 teaspoon cinnamon
1 tablespoon unsalted butter
½ lemon
¼ cup apple juice or juice concentrate

1. Preheat oven to 350°.
2. Core the apples, stopping ½ inch from the bottom. Peel skin off the top of the apple. Rub the cut surfaces with lemon, and squeeze just a little into the cored centers of the apples.
3. Mix together walnuts, raisins, dates, cinnamon, and butter. Stuff into hollow centers of apples.
4. Place apples in small baking dish. Pour juice into the bottom of the baking dish.
5. Bake, basting with the juices about every 10 minutes until apples are tender when pierced with a fork—about 45 to 50 minutes.
6. Serve in small bowls, and spoon liquid from the bottom of baking dish over apples.

TOTAL CALORIES PER SERVING: 330

% Calories Carbohydrates: 44
% Calories Protein: 9
% Calories Fat: 47

Total Cholesterol: 6 mg.
Total Sodium: 5 mg.
Total Potassium: 465 mg.
Total Calcium: 52 mg.
Total Fiber: 4 gm.

Dense and satisfying, carrot cake can be frosted for special occasions, or eaten plain as breakfast muffins or a snack. Either way, it's a great treat!

1¾ cup whole wheat pastry flour
2 teaspoons baking soda
2 teaspoons cinnamon
¼ teaspoon salt
¾ cup apple juice concentrate
1 cup raisins
3 eggs
2 teaspoons vanilla
½ cup buttermilk
¾ cup canola oil
2 cups carrots, finely grated
1 cup walnuts, coarsely chopped
½ cup unsweetened shredded coconut (optional)

1. Pre-heat oven to 350°. Sift together flour, baking soda, cinnamon, and salt. Set aside.
2. In a small saucepan, combine apple juice concentrate and raisins. Simmer for 10 minutes, or until liquid is reduced by about half. Cool and puree in a blender or food processor.
3. Blend eggs, buttermilk, oil, and vanilla until combined. Stir in carrots, walnut, coconut, apple juice and raisin mix.
3. Add dry ingredients. Stir until just combined.
4. Pour into 13 x 9, 10-inch round, or individual muffin cups. Bake cakes for 45 minutes or until a toothpick or knife inserted into the center comes out clean. Cupcakes need to bake approximately 25 minutes.

TOTAL CALORIES PER SERVING: 309

% Calories Carbohydrates: 41
% Calories Protein: 14
% Calories Fat: 46

Total Cholesterol: 83 mg.
Total Sodium: 137 mg.
Total Potassium: 422 mg.
Total Calcium: 110 mg.
Total Fiber: 0 gm.

Carrot Cake

Serves 8 to 10
Prep time: 20 minutes
Cooking time: 45 minutes

Cream Cheese Frosting

8 ounces cream cheese
4 tablespoons apple juice concentrate or honey
2 teaspoons vanilla

1. Whip cream cheese in blender, mixer, or food processor until light and fluffy. Add juice and vanilla, and process for another minute or so.
2. Spread on top of cake or cupcakes.

TOTAL CALORIES PER SERVING: 85

% Calories Carbohydrates: 10
% Calories Protein: 8
% Calories Fat: 82

Total Cholesterol: 25 mg.
Total Sodium: 68 mg.
Total Potassium: 42 mg.
Total Calcium: 19 mg.
Total Fiber: 0 gm.

The perfect summer dessert: sweet, juicy peaches in a flaky crust.

Crust:
2 cups whole wheat pastry flour
½ cup canola oil
¾ teaspoon salt
5 tablespoons ice water

1. Combine flour and salt in large bowl.
2. Beat oil and water until creamy.
3. Add flour mixture to liquid, and toss together with a fork.
4. Use your hands to shape dough into a flat disk.
5. Chill for at least 30 minutes.
6. Using the side of a glass or a rolling pin, roll out dough between two pieces of wax paper.
7. Press into a 9-inch pie dish or tin.

Filling:
4 cups peaches (about six large), peeled and sliced
2 egg whites
2 tablespoons flour
1 teaspoon lemon juice
½ teaspoon cinnamon
½ cup honey or ⅓ cup fruit juice concentrate—or, for a tart pie, use no sweetener at all!

1. Preheat oven to 400°.
2. Drop whole peaches into boiling water for one minute. Remove from heat, and rinse with cold water. This process will cause the peach skin to peel off easily. Slice peaches into ½-inch pieces. Sprinkle with lemon juice.
3. Add egg whites, flour, cinnamon, and sweetener to fruit.
4. Pour mixture into pie shell, and bake for 15 minutes. Reduce heat to 300°, and bake for 50 minutes longer. Serve hot or chilled. Delicious with vanilla frozen yogurt!

Fresh Peach Pie

Serves 6 to 8
Prep time: 1 hour

TOTAL CALORIES PER SERVING: 331

% Calories Carbohydrates: 57
% Calories Protein: 7
% Calories Fat: 37

Total Cholesterol: 0 mg.
Total Sodium: 63 mg.
Total Potassium: 280 mg.
Total Calcium: 26 mg.
Total Fiber: 0 gm.

Other Fruit Pies

The basic crust recipe given in the recipe for Fresh Peach Pie is useful for making any 9-inch, one-crust pie. Experiment with using different fruits and combinations of fruits. You will need 4 cups of fresh fruit or 3 cups of canned fruit. We suggest using fresh, organically grown fruit whenever possible. Some suggested fillings are listed below.

Instead of using flour and egg whites to thicken fruit mixture, you can use 3 tablespoons of quick-cooking tapioca. Allow the fruit and tapioca to rest together in a bowl for 15 minutes before filling pie shell and baking.

For a two-crust pie (a pie with a top), double the recipe and divide in half before chilling. For the top crust, roll out dough into an 11-inch disk. Place on fruit filled pie and, using just a little water on your fingertips, press and crimp the top and bottom crusts together around the edges. A one-crust pie has, of course, fewer calories and far less fat.

Already baked fruit pies freeze well, but microwaving them will make the crust soggy. Allow ample time to thaw, or heat in a 250° to 300° oven until it reaches the desired temperature.

Making fruit pies can be time-consuming, and tricky at first, but we think you will find them worth the effort.

Pears and Raspberries

2 cups sliced pears and 2 cups raspberries

TOTAL CALORIES PER SERVING: 64

% Calories Carbohydrates: 91
% Calories Protein: 3
% Calories Fat: 6

Total Cholesterol: 0 mg.
Total Sodium: 0 mg.
Total Potassium: 126 mg.
Total Calcium: 14 mg.
Total Fiber: 3 gm.

Apples and Pears

2 cups each sliced apples and pears

TOTAL CALORIES PER SERVING: 79

% Calories Carbohydrates: 93
% Calories Protein: 2
% Calories Fat: 5

Total Cholesterol: 0 mg.
Total Sodium: 1 mg.
Total Potassium: 138 mg.
Total Calcium: 11 mg.
Total Fiber: 3 gm.

Apples and Raisins

3½ cups apples and ½ cup raisins or currants

TOTAL CALORIES PER SERVING: 95

% Calories Carbohydrates: 95
% Calories Protein: 2
% Calories Fat: 3

Total Cholesterol: 0 mg.
Total Sodium: 2 mg.
Total Potassium: 184 mg.
Total Calcium: 12 mg.
Total Fiber: 0 gm.

Apricots and Cranberries

3 cups apricots and 1 cup cranberries (Very tart! Needs some sweetener.)

TOTAL CALORIES PER SERVING: 244

% Calories Carbohydrates: 94
% Calories Protein: 6
% Calories Fat: 1

Total Cholesterol: 0 mg.
Total Sodium: 0 mg.
Total Potassium: 87 mg.
Total Calcium: 5 mg.
Total Fiber: 0 gm.

2 cups whole wheat pastry flour
½ cup canola oil
¾ teaspoon salt
5 tablespoons ice water

Pie Crust

1. Combine flour and salt in large bowl.
2. Beat oil and water until creamy.
3. Add flour mixture to liquid, and toss together with a fork.
4. Use your hands to shape dough into a flat disk.
5. Chill for at least 30 minutes.
6. Using the side of a glass or a rolling pin, roll out dough between two pieces of wax paper.
7. Press into a 9-inch pie dish or tin.

TOTAL CALORIES PER SERVING: 1,752

% Calories Carbohydrates: 53
% Calories Protein: 44
% Calories Fat: 3

Total Cholesterol: 0 mg.
Total Sodium: 37 mg.
Total Potassium: 111 mg.
Total Calcium: 12 mg.
Total Fiber: 0 gm.

Joseph's Berry Pie

Serves 6 to 8
Prep time: 25 minutes
Waiting time: 2 hours

This pie is filled with deeply colored, sweet berries. Use fresh seasonal raspberries, blueberries, blackberries or strawberries.

Crust:
3 tablespoons apple juice concentrate
1 cup breakfast flake or grapenut cereal, crushed

1. Combine juice and cereal. Press into the bottom and sides of a 9-inch pie pan.
2. Bake for 10 minutes at 400°. Remove from oven and allow to cool.

Filling:
1 cup berry juice concentrate (raspberry, blueberry, or mixed berries)
2 cups water
1 cup fresh or frozen berries
1 cup unsweetened canned or frozen peaches, drained
6 tablespoons tapioca
2 envelopes unflavored gelatin

1. Let tapioca sit in water for 2 hours.
2. In a saucepan, combine juice concentrate, water/tapioca mixture, and gelatin. Boil for 10 minutes. Add fruit. Cook for 5 minutes if berries are fresh. Remove from heat, and pour fruit mixture into shell. Chill and serve.

TOTAL CALORIES PER SERVING: 157

% Calories Carbohydrates: 88
% Calories Protein: 11
% Calories Fat: 1

Total Cholesterol: 0 mg.
Total Sodium: 129 mg.
Total Potassium: 138 mg.
Total Calcium: 13 mg.
Total Fiber: 1 gm.

An old-fashioned chewy cookie made with juicy raisins and crunchy walnuts. Store cookies in an airtight container to ensure freshness.

½ cup fruit juice concentrate (white grape or apple)
½ cup chopped dates
½ cup canola oil
1 teaspoon vanilla extract
1 egg
¾ cup whole wheat flour
½ teaspoon baking soda
1½ teaspoons cinnamon
1½ cups rolled oats
½ cup raisins
½ cup walnuts, chopped

1. Preheat oven to 350°. Lightly grease a cookie sheet with oil or baking spray.
2. Heat fruit juice concentrate with dates over medium heat for 4 minutes. Stir constantly.
3. Combine juice, dates, oil, egg, and vanilla in a blender or food processor and puree.
4. Combine with flour, baking soda, cinnamon, and salt. Add rolled oats, raisins, and walnuts. Mix until fully combined.
5. Place tablespoons of dough about 2 inches apart on cookie sheet. Flatten tops of cookies. Bake for 10 to 12 minutes.
6. Allow cookies to cool briefly before removing them from cookie sheet.

Oatmeal Raisin Cookies

Makes 2 dozen
Prep time: 15 minutes
Baking time: 20 minutes

TOTAL CALORIES PER SERVING: 132

% Calories Carbohydrates: 49
% Calories Protein: 12
% Calories Fat: 39

Total Cholesterol: 11 mg.
Total Sodium: 165 mg.
Total Potassium: 141 mg.
Total Calcium: 102 mg.
Total Fiber: 2 gm.

Orange Poppy-Seed Cookies

Makes 2 dozen
Prep time: 15 minutes
Baking Time: 20 minutes

The flavors of orange, date, and poppy seeds merge together synergistically, creating a whole far greater than the sum of the parts. Perfect for a post-workout pick-me-up.

½ cup orange juice concentrate
½ cup dates, coarsely chopped
¼ cup butter
¼ cup canola oil
1 teaspoon vanilla
1 egg
½ teaspoon baking soda
1¾ cups whole wheat pastry flour
⅛ cup poppy seeds
1 teaspoon grated orange zest (optional)

1. Preheat oven to 350°.
2. In a saucepan, simmer dates and orange concentrate together for 4 minutes, stirring constantly. Remove from heat and allow to cool.
3. Puree in blender or food processor with butter, oil, vanilla and egg.
4. Return to large bowl, and add sifted flour and baking soda. Blend well. Fold in poppy seeds and orange zest.
5. Drop heaping teaspoons of batter on greased cookie sheet.
6. Bake for 8 to 10 minutes.

TOTAL CALORIES PER SERVING: 68

% Calories Carbohydrates: 52
% Calories Protein: 7
% Calories Fat: 40

Total Cholesterol: 2 mg.
Total Sodium: 16 mg.
Total Potassium: 67mg.
Total Calcium: 14 mg.
Total Fiber: 0 gm.

Carob may be no substitute for chocolate, but as a healthful, non-caffeine-free alternative, it blends nicely with peanut butter to create rich, chewy cookies that are easy to make.

8 tablespoons vegetable oil
½ cup peanut butter
4 tablespoons maple syrup
¼ cup apple juice concentrate
1 egg, lightly beaten
1 teaspoon vanilla
1¾ cups whole wheat pastry flour
¾ teaspoon baking soda

1. Preheat oven to 375°.
2. Combine peanut butter, maple syrup, apple juice concentrate and mix thoroughly.
3. Add egg and vanilla, and then flour and baking soda.
4. Drop rounded tablespoons of this mixture onto lightly greased baking sheets. Flatten tops using a fork or back of a teaspoon. Bake until golden in color—about 7 to 8 minutes.

TOTAL CALORIES PER SERVING: 86

% Calories Carbohydrates: 40
% Calories Protein: 7
% Calories Fat: 53

Total Cholesterol: 11 mg.
Total Sodium: 17 mg.
Total Potassium: 49 mg.
Total Calcium: 16 mg.
Total Fiber: 0 gm.

Peanut Butter Cookies with Carob Chips

Makes 2 dozen
Prep time: 15 minutes
Baking time: 20 minutes

Pear-Raspberry Crisp

Serves 4 to 6
Prep time: 20 minutes
Baking time: 40 minutes

The flavors of pear and raspberry complement each other wonderfully in this unusual fruit crisp.

Filling:
3 cups pears, peeled and sliced
1½ cups raspberries, fresh or frozen and drained

Topping:
¼ cup whole wheat pastry flour
¼ cup unbleached flour
6 tablespoons maple sugar granules
⅛ teaspoon sea salt
1 teaspoon cinnamon
¼ teaspoon ground nutmeg
3 tablespoons canola oil

1. Preheat oven to 325°.
2. Combine fruit and place in an 8- or 9-inch pan.
3. In a small bowl, combine flour, maple sugar, salt, cinnamon, and nutmeg. Drizzle oil over the flour mixture, and work into the flour with a fork until combined.
4. Distribute topping evenly over the fruit. Bake until the top is bubbly and lightly browned—about 40 minutes.

TOTAL CALORIES PER SERVING: 309

% Calories Carbohydrates: 72
% Calories Protein: 3
% Calories Fat: 25

Total Cholesterol: 0 mg.
Total Sodium: 17 mg.
Total Potassium: 295 mg.
Total Calcium: 88 mg.
Total Fiber: 4 gm.

Poached peaches are a simple, elegant dessert, delicious with peach or vanilla frozen yogurt.

2 large peaches
½ cup white wine
½ cup water
¼ apple or white grape juice concentrate
1 split vanilla bean, or 2 teaspoons vanilla
¼ medium-size orange, cut in half

1. Place wine, juice, vanilla, and orange (don't squeeze) in a saucepan. Slice peaches in half and remove pits.
2. Place peaches in liquid, cover, and cook on low heat for 20 to 25 minutes, or until peaches are tender. Pierce with fork to make sure the peaches are cooked all the way through. Fork will go through easily.
3. Remove peaches from liquid. Allow to cool. Using your hands, remove peach skin. Skin should come off easily.

TOTAL CALORIES PER SERVING: 129

% Calories Carbohydrates: 94
% Calories Protein: 4
% Calories Fat: 2

Total Cholesterol: 0 mg.
Total Sodium: 6 mg.
Total Potassium: 360 mg.
Total Calcium: 23 mg.
Total Fiber: 1 gm.

Poached Peaches

Serves 2
Prep time: 10 minutes
Cooking time: 25 minutes

Simple Applesauce

Makes 4 to 6 cups
Prep time: 15 minutes
Cooking time: 20 minutes

Serve plain or with simple breakfast crêpes, pancakes, or waffles.

6 Golden Delicious apples, peeled, cored and quartered
½ cup water
1 tablespoon cinnamon

For spicier sauce, add:
¼ teaspoon ground cloves, ¼ teaspoon nutmeg, and a dash of allspice, or use ½ teaspoon packaged pumpkin pie seasoning. Increase seasoning to taste.

For variety, cook apples with:
½ cup raspberries, or decrease apples by two and add two pears

1. In a saucepan, combine all ingredients.
2. Simmer covered for 20 minutes. Uncover and allow to cool in pan.
3. Depending on desired consistency, mash mixture with a fork or mix in blender.

TOTAL CALORIES PER SERVING: 83

% Calories Carbohydrates: 94
% Calories Protein: 1
% Calories Fat: 5

Total Cholesterol: 0 mg.
Total Sodium: 1 mg.
Total Potassium: 162 mg.
Total Calcium: 15 mg.
Total Fiber: 3 gm.

Here's a chilly, fruity summertime dessert that's a snap to make!

1 cup fresh strawberries
1 cup non-fat strawberry yogurt
1 teaspoon vanilla extract

(Add 2 tablespoons of apple juice concentrate for extra sweetness.)

---

1. Slice and then mash strawberries with a fork.
2. Mix fruit with yogurt, vanilla, and fruit concentrate.
3. Prepare in an ice cream maker and follow appliance directions, or freeze until solid and whip in a blender for 30 seconds until mixture has the consistency of a thick slush.
4. Serve plain or topped with toasted almonds.

TOTAL CALORIES PER SERVING: 109

% Calories Carbohydrates: 70
% Calories Protein: 27
% Calories Fat: 3

Total Cholesterol: 7 mg.
Total Sodium: 81 mg.
Total Potassium: 426 mg.
Total Calcium: 220 mg.
Total Fiber: 1 gm.

Strawberry Frozen Yogurt

Serves 2
Prep time: 10 minutes

Winter Fruit Salad

Serves 2
Prep time: 10 minutes

Serve topped with non-fat vanilla yogurt and chopped walnuts.

1 apple
1 pear
1 banana
1 orange
¾ cup green grapes
½ cup dark raisins or currants

1. Peel fruit. Remove seeds and cores. Cut apple, orange, and pear into small cubes. Slice banana. Slice grapes in halves.
2. Combine fruit in a large bowl with raisins. Refrigerate until time to serve.
3. Top with yogurt and walnuts and serve immediately.

TOTAL CALORIES PER SERVING: 349

% Calories Carbohydrates: 94
% Calories Protein: 3
% Calories Fat: 3

Total Cholesterol: 0 mg.
Total Sodium: 8 mg.
Total Potassium: 851 mg.
Total Calcium: 47 mg.
Total Fiber: 7 gm.

10

DRINKS

Banana-Raspberry Breakfast Shake

Serves 1 to 2
Prep time: 10 minutes

A thick breakfast drink with the consistency of a milk-shake. For variety, try it with non-fat milk in place of juice.

1 whole banana, sliced
1 cup fresh or frozen raspberries
1 cup apple juice
4 ice cubes
protein powder (optional)

Combine ingredients in blender until it reaches the consistency of a shake—about 30 seconds to 1 minute. Serve.

TOTAL CALORIES PER SERVING: 161

% Calories Carbohydrates: 86
% Calories Protein: 9
% Calories Fat: 5

Total Cholesterol: 0 mg.
Total Sodium: 30 mg.
Total Potassium: 497 mg.
Total Calcium: 25 mg.
Total Fiber: 4 gm.

This spicy cider is particularly comforting on a cold winter evening.

1 32-ounce bottle good quality apple cider
2 cinnamon sticks
1 tablespoon whole cloves

1. Combine all ingredients in a large soup pot. Heat, covered, over low heat for 15 to 20 minutes.
2. Serve hot in mugs or cups.

TOTAL CALORIES PER SERVING: 119

% Calories Carbohydrates: 96
% Calories Protein: 1
% Calories Fat: 3

Total Cholesterol: 0 mg.
Total Sodium: 9 mg.
Total Potassium: 305 mg.
Total Calcium: 27 mg.
Total Fiber: 0 gm.

Hot Apple Cider

Makes 4 cups
Prep time: 20 minutes

Tropical Fruit Shake

Serves 1 to 2
Prep time: 10 minutes

A delicious citrus shake for any time of day.

1 banana
½ cup orange juice
½ cup pineapple (canned or fresh, unsweetened)
6 ice cubes
protein powder (optional)

Combine ingredients and blend until smooth. Serve.

TOTAL CALORIES PER SERVING: 120

% Calories Carbohydrates: 82
% Calories Protein: 12
% Calories Fat: 6

Total Cholesterol: 0 mg.
Total Sodium: 28 mg.
Total Potassium: 423 mg.
Total Calcium: 13 mg.
Total Fiber: 1 gm.

Watermelon Slush

Nothing is more refreshing or thirst-quenching after a hard workout on a hot summer day than fresh watermelon. Try this the next time the mercury rises.

5 cups seedless watermelon, cubed
2 tablespoons lemon juice
8 ice cubes

Puree in blender, and serve.

Serves 1 to 2
Prep time: 10 minutes.

TOTAL CALORIES PER SERVING: 129

% Calories Carbohydrates: 82
% Calories Protein: 7
% Calories Fat: 11

Total Cholesterol: 0 mg.
Total Sodium: 8 mg.
Total Potassium: 465 mg.
Total Calcium: 33 mg.
Total Fiber: 1 gm.

11

SAUCES AND DRESSINGS

Fat-Free Tomato Sauce

Makes 4 cups
Prep time: 20 minutes
Cooking time:
20 to 30 minutes

A wonderful, light sauce for pizza, packed with crisp vegetables for an appealing flavor and texture.

1 onion, chopped
1 zucchini, chopped
2 cups broccoli, cut into florets
1 green pepper, seeded and chopped
1 cup fresh mushrooms, cleaned and sliced
3 large cloves garlic, minced
1 28-ounce can tomatoes
½ cup black olives, pitted and halved

1. In a saucepan with vegetable steamer, steam onion, zucchini, broccoli, and green pepper until vegetables (except mushrooms) are tender—about 10 minutes.
2. In a large pot, combine mushrooms, garlic, tomatoes, and olives with steamed vegetables. Cook over a low heat for 20 to 30 minutes, until flavors are well combined and the juice from the tomatoes has been reduced by 25%.

TOTAL CALORIES: 81

% Calories Carbohydrates: 56
% Calories Protein: 13
% Calories Fat: 31

Total Cholesterol: 0 mg.
Total Sodium: 225 mg.
Total Potassium: 517 mg.
Total Calcium: 62 mg.
Total Fiber: 2 gm.

Lime-Dill Dressing

Makes ⅓ cup
Prep time: 10 minutes

Serve on salad greens, or use as a marinade for fish.

4 tablespoons fresh lime juice
2 teaspoons grated lime zest
½ teaspoon Dijon mustard
½ teaspoon ground pepper
¼ teaspoon sea salt
1 teaspoon dried or 1 tablespoon fresh, dill, minced
¼ cup canola oil

1. Mix together lime juice, lime zest, mustard, and pepper in a medium-size bowl.
2. Slowly blend in oil, all the time mixing vigorously, and combine to a thick, even consistency.

TOTAL CALORIES: 126

% Calories Carbohydrates: 13
% Calories Protein: 85
% Calories Fat: 2

Total Cholesterol: 0 mg.
Total Sodium: 80 mg.
Total Potassium: 24 mg.
Total Calcium: 14 mg.
Total Fiber: 0 gm.

Onion-Herb Yogurt Dip

Makes 1 cup
Prep time: 10 minutes

A great dip for fresh vegetables that may also be used as a healthy alternative to sour cream to fill baked potatoes.

1 cup non-fat yogurt
¼ cup finely minced green onions
2 tablespoons lime juice
2 tablespoons fresh cilantro or coriander, minced
1 clove garlic, crushed
sea salt and ground black or cayenne pepper

Combine ingredients in a medium-size bowl, and serve chilled.

TOTAL CALORIES: 23

% Calories Carbohydrates: 47
% Calories Protein: 18
% Calories Fat: 35

Total Cholesterol: 4 mg.
Total Sodium: 301 mg.
Total Potassium: 72 mg.
Total Calcium: 42 mg.
Total Fiber: 0 gm.

Raita is a tart mixture of yogurt and cold vegetables from India. We suggest eating it as a starter salad or snack with pita or other flat bread.

1 medium firm tomato, chopped
into ¼- to ½-inch chunks
1 small cucumber, peeled and chopped
into ¼- to ½-inch chunks
1 or 2 scallions, chopped
1 tablespoon fresh mint, chopped
1½ cups non-fat plain yogurt
¼ teaspoon ground cumin (found in the spice section of the market)

Combine vegetables in a medium-size bowl. Gently blend in yogurt. Serve chilled.

TOTAL CALORIES: 245

% Calories Carbohydrates: 10
% Calories Protein: 3
% Calories Fat: 87

Total Cholesterol: 22 mg.
Total Sodium: 95 mg.
Total Potassium: 885 mg.
Total Calcium: 283 mg.
Total Fiber: 2 gm.

Raita

Makes 2 cups
Prep time 15 minutes

Raspberry Marinade for Chicken

Makes marinade for one whole chicken
Prep time: 10 minutes

You can use this marinade with barbecued or baked chicken. It gives chicken a tart, fruity taste that makes it great in a formal setting or cold on summer picnics.

⅓ cup raspberry vinegar (available in the gourmet section of your supermarket)
½ cup white wine
¼ cup olive oil
juice of ½ lemon
½ cup mashed raspberries (fresh or frozen)
2 shallots
freshly ground pepper to taste

Combine all of the ingredients in a bowl, and mix vigorously to combine. Marinate chicken pieces for 1 to 4 hours.

TOTAL CALORIES: 606

% Calories Carbohydrates: 18
% Calories Protein: 1
% Calories Fat: 81

Total Cholesterol: 0 mg.
Total Sodium: 5 mg.
Total Potassium: 291 mg.
Total Calcium: 32 mg.
Total Fiber: 3 gm.

To use as a sandwich filling, add only half the amount of yogurt.

1 6-ounce can salmon, packed in water
1 8-ounce container plain non-fat yogurt
5 olives, finely chopped
ground black pepper to taste

1. Drain salmon.
2. Mix thoroughly with yogurt.
3. Add olives, and serve with vegetables or crackers.

TOTAL CALORIES: 399

% Calories Carbohydrates: 14
% Calories Protein: 34
% Calories Fat: 53

Total Cholesterol: 113 mg.
Total Sodium: 366 mg.
Total Potassium: 880 mg.
Total Calcium: 332 mg.
Total Fiber: 1 gm.

Salmon Dip

Makes 1½ cups
Prep time: 10 minutes

Balsamic Vinaigrette

Makes ⅔ cup
Prep time: 10 minutes

Balsamic vinegar is derived from the unfermented juice of the white trebbiano grape, and is made in Italy. It is a fruity, tart, richly flavored vinegar that makes delicious dressings and marinades.

4 tablespoons balsamic vinegar
1 tablespoon Dijon mustard
1 clove garlic, minced or pressed
½ cup extra virgin olive oil
½ teaspoon ground black pepper

1. Combine vinegar, mustard, and garlic. Stir vigorously.
2. While stirring constantly, slowly pour in olive oil until mixture thickens and oil is fully incorporated.

TOTAL CALORIES: 982

% Calories Carbohydrates: 1
% Calories Protein: 1
% Calories Fat: 99

Total Cholesterol: 0 mg.
Total Sodium: 206 mg.
Total Potassium: 43 mg.
Total Calcium: 28 mg.
Total Fiber: 0 gm.

VINAIGRETTE DRESSINGS FOR SALADS

A basic vinaigrette dressing can be made with just about any type of vinegar by simply adjusting the seasonings to complement its special flavor. Be creative! Try raspberry or blueberry vinegars with honey and tarragon, champagne vinegar, rice vinegar with low-sodium soy sauce and grated ginger, or simple white-wine vinegar with mixed Italian seasonings and a teaspoon of lemon juice. Below are some combinations we particularly like.

White-Wine Vinaigrette

Makes ⅔ cup
Prep time: 10 minutes

White-wine vinegar is made from fermented white wine. This is a slightly sweet, slightly tart, basic dressing.

4 tablespoons white-wine tarragon vinegar
1 teaspoon honey (optional)
1 teaspoon dried or 2 tablespoons fresh, tarragon
½ teaspoon sea salt
½ teaspoon ground black pepper
½ cup extra virgin olive oil

Mix together all ingredients except for oil. Add oil slowly.

TOTAL CALORIES: 968

% Calories Carbohydrates: 1
% Calories Protein: 1
% Calories Fat: 99

Total Cholesterol: 0 mg.
Total Sodium: 196 mg.
Total Potassium: 61 mg.
Total Calcium: 20 mg.
Total Fiber: 0 gm.

Red-Wine Vinaigrette

Makes ½ cup
Prep time: 10 minutes

A more intensely flavored vinegar than that made from white wine, red-wine vinegar makes an ideal vinaigrette for romaine lettuce salads, broccoli, or pasta salads.

4 tablespoons red-wine vinegar
1 tablespoon lemon juice
¼ teaspoon sea salt
½ teaspoon black pepper
¼ cup fresh minced parsley
¼ cup extra virgin olive oil

Mix together all ingredients except for oil. Add oil slowly.

TOTAL CALORIES: 495

% Calories Carbohydrates: 2
% Calories Protein: 0
% Calories Fat: 98

Total Cholesterol: 0 mg.
Total Sodium: 106 mg.
Total Potassium: 113 mg.
Total Calcium: 22 mg.
Total Fiber: 0 gm.

This marinade is meant for meaty white fish such as halibut, swordfish, or salmon.

⅓ cup white wine
½ cup white-wine vinegar
¼ cup olive oil
3 shallots, or 2 tablespoons onion, coarsely chopped
1 tablespoon dried, or 2 tablespoons fresh, parsley or cilantro
1 teaspoon dried, or 3 tablespoons fresh, thyme

1. Combine all ingredients in a shallow bowl. Mix thoroughly. Add cleaned fish. Allow to marinate for no more than 30 minutes.
2. Marinated fish can be grilled, baked, or broiled.

TOTAL CALORIES: 567

% Calories Carbohydrates: 13
% Calories Protein: 1
% Calories Fat: 86

Total Cholesterol: 0 mg.
Total Sodium: 21 mg.
Total Calcium: 78 mg.
Total Fiber: 0 gm.

White Wine Thyme Marinade for Fish

Makes 1 cup
Prep time: 10 minutes

Easy Tomato Salsa

Prep time: 15 minutes

3 large ripe tomatoes, chopped
¼ cup onion, minced
3 tablespoons cilantro, chopped
1 clove garlic, minced
2 teaspoons olive oil
2 teaspoons lemon juice
sea salt and pepper to taste

Combine ingredients in a medium-size bowl.
Mix thoroughly.

TOTAL CALORIES 168

% Calories Carbohydrates: 51
% Calories Protein: 10
% Calories Fat: 39

Total Cholesterol: 0 mg.
Total Sodium: 422 mg.
Total Potassium: 1024 mg.
Total Calcium: 90 mg.
Total Fiber: 3 gm.

INDEX

The Human Fuel Handbook

The Human Fuel Handbook is Health For Life's guide to peak performance nutrition, written especially for the dedicated athlete. Nutrient by nutrient, you'll discover how protein, carbohydrate, fat, minerals and vitamins function in your body...and why much of what you've heard about these substances is wrong. You'll get the real story on energy production, sports drinks, free-form amino acids, B-15, ginseng, Omega-3, steroid replacements, and much more! *Over 300 pages.*

Legendary Abs

Featuring the Synergism Principle, **Legendary Abs II** guarantees rock-hard, well-defined abdominals in just 6 minutes a day! See results within two weeks, or your money back. Not isometrics or some other supposed shortcut, Legendary Abs II is just good science applied to bodybuilding. Over 300,000 copies sold worldwide! *A 48 p. illustrated manual.*

SynerAbs: 6 Minutes to a Flatter Stomach

Women's edition of the **Legendary Abs II** program. Guarantees a firm, well-toned midsection in just 6 minutes a day! Ten levels of routines, from beginning to advanced. *A 48 p. illustrated manual.*

Transfigure I: 9 Minutes to the Ultimate Buttocks and Thighs

Transfigure is a revolutionary, high-gear system of buttock and thigh conditioning, keyed to a woman's specific aesthetic goals and based on sound biomechanical principles. Forget doing hundreds of ineffective leg exercises. Get set for the fastest results you've ever experienced, with routines that allow you to take control of your body and create the lean, shapely form you want!

Transfigure includes separate routines involving body weight exercise, light resistance exercise—even competition bodybuilding work. Whether you're working for general firmness and tone, or strength and high definition, **Transfigure** is your formula for the ultimate lower body, *in just 9 minutes! 126 pp. Over 200 photographs.*

Transfigure II: For the Ultimate Upper Body

Part two of our specially designed training program for women, **Transfigure II** adds the finishing touches to the ultimate physique. It concentrates on two areas that make the biggest difference in the shape and definition of the upper body: the backs of the upper arms and the chest. It also promotes attractive, balanced development of the shoulders, back and biceps. From light-resistance exercises all the way to competition bodybuilding work...*you* select the intensity that matches your experience and goals. For all-around firmness, tone and shapely definition. *130 pages, over 100 photographs.*

Secrets of Advanced Bodybuilders

What **Legendary Abs** and **SynerAbs** do for abdominal conditioning, **Secrets of Advanced Bodybuilders** does for your whole workout! **Secrets** explains how to apply the Synergism Principle to training back, chest, delts, biceps, triceps, quads, and hamstrings. It unlocks the secrets of the Optimum Workout and shows you how to develop the best routines for *you*—with your particular goals, strengths, and body structure.

Get the *ultimate* program. Plus, learn... ❑ a new back exercise that will pile on the mass and increase power without putting harmful stress on your lower back ❑ a technique for making Leg Extensions 200% more intense by targeting both inner *and outer* quads ❑ the shift in position that cranks Pull-Up and Pull-

Down exercises to three times normal intensity ❑ a *body weight* triceps exercise that will be "a growing experience" even for someone who's been training for years ❑ a *body weight* lat exercise that will mass up your back faster than you would have believed possible ❑ a special shoulder set that's more effective than most entire delt routines—also—❑ the best way to integrate your other athletic endeavors—running, cycling, stretching, mountain climbing, martial arts, etc.—into your routine to create the optimum overall program ❑ techniques for maximizing the effectiveness of *all* exercises you do, not just those in the course...and much, much more! *Stop working harder than you need to to get the results you want. Put the* **Secrets of Advanced Bodybuilders** *to work for you today!* 158 pp. Over 300 illustrations.

MAX O2: The Complete Guide to Synergistic Aerobic Training

Maximize your aerobic capacity faster and with less work than ever before! **MAX O2** represents an exciting new breakthrough in aerobic traing. It offers a completely new perspective on the combined effect of VO2 max and lactate threshold—and on the vital role this effect plays in optimum aerobic conditioning. Learn: ❑ How the F.I.T. principle (Frequency, Intensity, and Time) can help you experience the same progress in your cardiovascular training as in other parts of your workout ❑ How to build aerobics into any conditioning program (Bodybuilders: here's the secret to dropping bodyfat without losing muscle mass!) ❑ Benefits and myths of cross-training ❑ How to avoid injuries that can be caused by high-intensity aerobic work ❑ Losing weight ❑ Endurance events ❑ and much, much more! *Over 200 pages, illustrated.*

SynerShape: A Scientific Weight Loss Guide

We're surrounded by weight loss myths. Crash diets. Spot reducing. Exotic herbs. Still, most plans fail, and most people who lose weight gain it back again. Is there really an honest, effective solution? **Yes!** **SynerShape** represents the next generation in awareness of how the body gains and metabolizes fat. It synthesizes the most recent findings on nutrition, exercise, and psychology into a TOTAL program, offering you the tools you need to shape the body you want. **SynerShape** works. Let it work for *you!* A 24 p. *illustrated manual.*

The Psychology of Weight Loss

This special program-on-tape picks up where **SynerShape** leaves off. Noted psychologist Carol Landesman explores eating problems and *solutions* based on the latest research into human behavior and metabolism. Then, through a series of exercises, she helps you begin to heal the emotional conflicts behind your weight problem. **The Psychology of Weight Loss** is a unique program that brings the power of the therapy process into the privacy of your home. *A 90-minute guided introspection. On audio cassette.*

For price and order information, or
to receive a FREE copy of the Health For Life Catalogue
call 1-800-874-5339
or write us at...

Health For Life
Suite 483
8033 Sunset Blvd.
Los Angeles, CA 90046

Notes

Notes

Notes

Notes

Notes

Notes

Notes

Notes

741102